Crumbs Along the Broken Path

One Story at a Time

Dear Debbie
May you gather
many rich crumbles
along your path!
Uma

Crumbs Along the Broken Path

One Story at a Time

verna
bowman

Ampelos Press
Lansdale, PA

Crumbs Along the Broken Path – One Story at a Time
Copyright © 2014 by Verna Bowman

Published by Ampelos Press
951 Anders Road, Lansdale, PA 19446
http://www.writehisanswer.com/ampelospress

Editing and Typesetting: Marlene Bagnull
Proofreader: Christy Distler
Cover Design: Jo Lauter and Marlene Bagnull
Cover Photo and basket: Ann Edmonds
Blackbird: Marji Stevens
Verna Bowman's photo: Littlewing Studio Photography
Clipart on page 159 by Bing Clipart, www.wickedwriter.blogspot.com

ISBN: 978-0-9960095-0-8

Printed in the U.S.A.

Dedicated to the One
who wrote my life story

Verna has lived turbulence. Verna has lived disruption. Verna has lived disappointment. Most importantly, Verna has lived and continues to live in the peace and purpose ministered by the Lord Jesus. She's not just a survivor, but she is a learner, a disciple of Christ Jesus, and a faithful communicator of God's goodness and truth.

Pastor John H. C. Niederhaus
Immanuel Leidy's Church
Souderton, PA

Contents

There were two gates to enter the property
of my childhood home. One gate was narrow
leading to home. It was hard to open,
I had to kick the bottom and push against it.
The other was a wide gate to enter the driveway.
This one seemed to open of its own accord.
I used the wide gate—it was easier.

Introduction

We all have a story that tells of the path we've taken while trying to find our way. Early on, I took the broad road that leads to nowhere. We may have crossed paths.

Life is full of unplanned detours taking us to places where we feel there is nowhere to turn. Walking over broken pieces of life can lead to a painful dead end. You may be there now. Whether our struggles are similar or different, we all want to wind up in the same destination—wholeness.

For a long time the world's scenery distracted me. I wasn't watching where I was going until I found something along the path to lead me in a different direction.

Crumbs.

Remember the dark tale of Hansel and Gretel? They followed intentionally scattered bread crumbs to try to find their way. Unfortunately, the birds came along and ate the pieces of bread. The abandoned children became hopelessly lost. They needed a route leading to hope. So did I. The darker my journey became, the harder it was to see anything except what was before me—more darkness. Finally I came to a narrow road littered with crumbs, placed there on purpose by a sovereign Father.

Crumbs Along the Broken Path is the fruit of what I gathered along the way. Crumbs are symbolic of the things God uses in our lives, the good and the not-so-good, to get our attention and keep us on track.

Piles of journals condensed into a collection of a few short stories on the following pages were originally intended as a way of recording God's faithfulness for my children and grandchildren. Stories—just scattered stories, not necessarily in any semblance of order. However, years in women's ministry have taken me to the deep heart of the wounded. And so I'm sharing my story to offer hope to those lost in the dark forest of their own story.

We can find our way when we stop to gather the sovereign crumbs purposely placed on our path.

May we find them together.

*If you don't know where you're going,
any road will get you there.*

Lewis Carroll

How far is heaven from earth?
Heaven is as close as our mind. Mine was far off
on the path from Woodstock to awestruck
by the God of Wonder.

Woodstock
to
Wonderstruck

Growing up in an age of innocence followed by one of the most violent decades in American history was a bitter mix. The 1960s were a major turning point in the history of our country, when social upheaval dominated the landscape. Having one foot in the fifties and one in the sixties became a difficult path to walk.

Where were you when the world spun out of control?

I was there.

There is a time for all of us when the clock stopped with the unforgettable moments that changed our world. I'm old enough to remember when the first man entered space, and a few years later when another actually took a walk on the moon.

I was sixteen years old, sitting in a Philadelphia deli, when the shocking broadcast came over a black and white TV that President Kennedy had been assassinated. I was there when Martin Luther King had a dream. Why would anyone want to kill the little bit of peace we had in the world?

And I was pregnant with my second child when I got the call that a close classmate had been killed in Vietnam. On Christmas day. I was twenty. So was he.

Our world didn't make sense. The music of the era defined the heart of the counterculture singing of freedom, rights for all races, and the right not to go to wars where we didn't belong. At a time when America was deeply divided, during the summer of '69 a half-million kids gathered in the fields of Yasgur's hog farm in upstate New York for a three day peace and music festival... Woodstock. It was a time to make love, not war. And yes, I was part of the incense, love beads, flower-in-a-gun-barrel hippie movement.

My world didn't make sense. By this time, I had left school, married at seventeen, and had two babies. I loved being a mom, but it didn't take long for my troubled marriage to become unbearable. The black hole I had gotten myself into kept getting deeper and darker. Dreams burst, life broke, and I fell through the cracks.

Disillusioned and free-spirited, I couldn't wait to go to Woodstock and find peace, if only for three days. The promo on the ticket had a dove perched on an acoustic guitar fret—a portrait of peace. That's how I saw it, anyway.

It was a time when people seemed to be on a quest for spirituality and consciousness. They looked toward the Eastern mystics for inner peace and tranquility or inside themselves to "tune in and drop out" with Timothy Leary's philosophy. Me, too.

Traveling light with only a backpack, but heavy with life's baggage, I was on my way somewhere going nowhere on the back of a Harley. Joni Mitchell sang her Woodstock anthem of getting your soul free and *coming upon a child of God, going on down the road.* Everyone must be a child of God, I thought. After all, Jesus taught about peace and love and getting back to the garden. Maybe I was going the right way.

However, it didn't take long for me to discover there wasn't enough music to find peace or enough rain to be cleansed. I brought home the same stuff I left with.

Much has happened since the late sixties. I ask my children and grandchildren the milestones in their lifetime. I hang on each answer—from the amazing changes of President Reagan bringing down the Wall, to the rage of terrorists bringing down the Towers.

Looking back on the turbulent times of my world then and the world I live in now, I wonder why... Why did hundreds of thousands of young people congregating in a mud-drenched field and dealing with food shortages, unsanitary conditions, and torrential rain, not have so much as a fight break out? Why did everyone help one another?

Today we're at war with ourselves. Our children aren't safe in theaters or classrooms without being gunned down.

We all need a Woodstock. Agree?

Contrary to the belief of those who raise an eyebrow when looking through the decadence of documentaries, this was not simply a mess of unwashed, doped-out freaks dancing in the mire. It was deeper than the mud.

August 2014 will be the forty-fifth anniversary of the music festival, and I continue to believe everyone has their own Woodstock along the way as they look for what they can't find.

Five years ago, I returned to what was once Yasgur's

farm in Bethel. Strangely enough, the word *bethel* means sacred ground, house of God. It definitely was a place I stopped along my sacred path leading to the house of God, although it took a long time and many turns in the road to get there. Now erected on neatly manicured fields stands the Bethel Woods Festival for the Arts, a museum filled with ghosts of Woodstock past.

I am one of the ghosts.

Crumbs

I fell into the trap of a generation and personal circumstances. The tumultuous happenings in our world and within my home had me chasing something I couldn't find.

For me, the sixties were more than a moment in time. Instead it was a time of a historical shift in thinking, taking me on a panoramic view of where I once visited in life to where I came to stay.

While chasing music and futility, the faithful God of heaven was chasing me. Six years after Woodstock, wallowing in muddy grace, I caught a glimpse of crumbs leading to Glory and my life changed forever. I found the true peace I had been searching for.

Do you believe God can re-do you?

But now in Christ Jesus
you who formerly were far off
have been brought near by the blood of Christ.
Ephesians 2:13

If only we could return to the innocence.
My innocence. Before I took the wide road.

Back to the Garden

As a young girl, I spent a lot of time with my paternal grandmother. Our chats inside the gates of her wisteria-filled garden speak loud to me today. Whenever I pass the acrid scent of boxwood, I can hear her voice and see her standing tall with a hoe in one hand and a watering can in the other. The old rusty can is split from age. It no longer holds water, but it still contains all of her stories that can never leak out. I remember each one.

Grandma would tell me what it was like growing up during the turn of the century. Her Irish immigrant mother died when Emily Rose was very young, leaving her and her brothers and sisters to be raised by a strong-handed father. He taught her to be self-sufficient and strong. She was.

She married teenage-young and raised a large brood of eight while running a huckstering business and owning one of the only icehouses in Philadelphia. She was proud to tell me how she threw huge blocks of ice onto the delivery wagons.

No, she wasn't the classic and spectacled bedtime-story-granny, but she was mine.

I loved her raw honesty and how she didn't speak to me like I was a child. In fact, most times she cussed like her sailor son, not paying attention to tender ears.

I heard her stories so often I could recite them. Her love of flowers dominated many of them. With a Gaelic lilt in her voice she'd say, "Flowers should never be white. We need color in our lives. Flowers tell a story, some stately and tall, and some wilted by life. You need to decide which one you'll be, Verna Rose."

My grandmother knew the pain of life. Acquainted with the sorrow of losing stillborn twins, a five-year-old son, and another son who never returned from World War II, she made no apology for who she was and how she thought. I almost understood the giant walls that kept her heart safe.

With Grandma, you weren't picked up and pampered after a fall. Instead, she would brush me off and re-twist my auburn braids so tight I thought I'd scream as she reminded me to *stand straight, hang tough, no tears*. It didn't help that from a young age I was told I was "just like Grandma Rose." I heard it enough to make it true and thought I should live up to it. I believed I must have inherited the survival seed by way of genetics.

For a time, her words got me through a hurtful childhood dealing with my dad's alcoholism. Strong, stoic, even coarse, my father was much like his mother. I believed he was invincible. He had a fondness for Irish whiskey that intruded on the peace in our home, sometimes making it tough to cope. A towering man, he created a "don't mess with me" reputation, but within the deep places of his heart was a loving, hardworking, and decent man. One who taught me to stand up to life's punches.

16

My grandmother's hang-tough philosophy almost got me through my difficult teenage years. For me, high school was a painful place filled with rumor giants. I became one of the mean girls. When my behavior became uncontrollable, I was soon asked to leave. Permanently. Rebellion took me to the starting line of a very wide road that would soon drop me into the dark.

I thought Grandma's crude mentoring was the only way to get through sadness. It seemed to work for her. *Stand straight, hang tough, no tears.*

Life became harder after leaving home at seventeen. I thought I could do it better on my own than what had been done for me. So, I got a job as a shampoo-girl and went to an academy to become a hair stylist. I soon found the profession didn't merge well with my poor attitude, because I didn't like people. *Really.*

There have been times in the past half-century when I've been tempted to go back to the garden and remember my grandmother's words and try her way...again. Her influence disguised a shy child with "hang tough, no tears" self-survival.

I'm grateful for the strong grandmother and father who instilled iron within me at a young age that helped me get through the hard times. God knows what we need before we realize our need for Him.

It took a dramatic shift in life to learn a holy lesson that the One who did hang tough on a cross was my true source of strength. He showed me the only way to get through the unbearable is to *bend low, humble myself, and cry out.*

If Grandma were here today, I'd join her in the bitter mix of wisteria and boxwoods to share some of my war stories. And with a knowing that comes from living life, I'd tell her, "Not this time, Grandma. I can't fix, control, or bully my way through this kind of pain. I need something bigger than me. I *am* strong, and I got that way because of what is written in the Bible. My hope is to be remembered as one of the flowers we spoke of—the stately, colorful one unwilted by life."

Crumbs

Although my grandmother taught me to be tough, self-survival didn't always work. It merely disguised my hurt, but couldn't bring healing. I learned to stuff the painful experiences as deep as the seeds in her garden. Later in life it gave root to the sin of self-protection.

Sometimes the well-meaning words spoken over us as children are the crumbs we gather. They can be the beginning of leading us in the wrong direction.

What is the good-bad teaching
you've had to work through?

Speak to the earth and it will teach you...
Who among all these does not know
That the hand of the LORD has done this?
Job 12:8–9 NKJV

Inspired by the faith of one woman
and the grieving cry of another, the faithful prayers
of a young girl developed into a life of intercession
for those who hurt. A lifetime of circumstances
recycled an unbeliever into a prayer warrior.

Recycled Faith

During the wholesome era of *Leave it to Beaver* and *Father Knows Best*, when kids were kids, moms were moms, and fathers knew best, I was a kid. Back then a rare few real-life families resembled these fiction families, but things were not that way for most of us. I guess my home-life was more of a reality show.

Can you relate?

The simpler times on the 50's planet were very different from today. When we went into the woods to pick berries, we were concerned about snakes, not pedophiles or kidnappers. There was always a neighborhood Kool-Aid mom ready with a cold drink and a bandage when we skinned our knee. There was never a lawsuit if you fell out of a neighbor's tree. Our curfew was the flash of fireflies sending us home before dusk became darkness. And we could play outside alone…without worry.

In days gone-by, the American way was quiet reverence for God and country, no matter how you believed. I can't remember anyone saying anything disrespectful about the Almighty or the President. Every morning our school day opened with hand over heart, pledging allegiance to the flag. Bowed heads and folded hands sent up a prayer to "our Father who art in heaven" from our two-room public schoolhouse. Every-one-of-us.

Within my home was a different story. There was no mention of God. My mom had a distant belief, but my dad declared himself an atheist more than once. I didn't have much exposure to church as a child except when a parent rounded up the kids at the sound of the church bell to drop us off for Sunday School. However, sweet memories remain of my mother and I walking up to the neighborhood church for Easter Sunday services.

My close childhood friend lived in a storybook house securely surrounded by a white picket fence. Raised by a devout Hungarian Catholic mother with a tenacious faith, Mary Magdalena's (yes, this is her real name) homelife was very different from mine.

Mrs. Csoky was one of my favorite friend-moms. She has left tracks on my heart to this day. More dedicated than the mailman, she didn't let rain, wind, sleet, or snow keep her from going to mass at her church more than two miles away. She trudged through snow drifted high in the dead of winter, and in the heat of summer she rode her daughter's bicycle. From my bedroom window I watched her go on her faithful trek and hoped one day I could believe in anything, even Elvis, that would generate that kind of effort and loyalty.

When I was twelve, I had a brief meeting with Mrs. Csoky's God.

Coming home from school one day, I hesitated at the top of the hill when I heard a woman crying. As I came closer to the open window, I heard sobs slowly turn into a guttural wail. I thought something must be terribly wrong, but I was afraid to knock at the door so I ran home to tell my mom. She told me a car had struck Mrs. Carson's fourteen-year-old son while he was riding his bicycle. He was thrown forty-two feet and was not expected to live.

The sounds of Mrs. Carson's broken heart broke mine that night. Lying awake, I wondered what a twelve-year-old could do to help. I thought I had to get to the place where Mrs. Csoky went and ask her God to allow Bobby to live. So, the next day and the days that followed for three weeks, I rode my bike to her church. Stained-glass windows and rich fragrance of incense made it seem like a hallowed place. God must be there, I thought. I prayed to a God I didn't know, but One who knew me. Bobby lived, and within a few months was well enough to return to school and pull my braids.

I believed God must've heard my feeble prayer.

Unfortunately, this life lesson became a faded memory, and for many years I put my faith in everything but Mrs. Csoky's God.

Looking back on my two-wheel adventure when I met Him as a brief acquaintance, I think of all that happened in-between. It's been well over fifty years ago since the Father bent down to listen to the prayer of a twelve-year-old girl who heard the cry of a mother. Even though "back home" is over thirty miles away, I continue to stop in every now and again to pray at the little church in Trevose. Returning to the hallowed silence, I sit in the same time-worn pew where I prayed for a grieving mother. Who knew I'd become that mom who would be praying for my own children enough to add to the wear of the pew.

The same God hears and answers. Still.

Crumbs

I had no spiritual background of my own, but I was curious about the faith I observed in my friend's mother. Limited by ignorance and age, I thought going to the church she faithfully visited might make the difference in a desperate situation.

The early crumbs I gathered slipped through my fingers. They were trampled on the path going my way after the brief encounter. It took years before I understood that God knows us before we know Him. His grace had me keep a portion to lead me back to the place where they were found.

Has there ever been a time when you recognized that God knew you before you knew Him?

"Before I formed you in the womb I knew you."
Jeremiah 1:5

22

As a young teen, I narrowly escaped the attack
of an evil predator who later became identified
as a convicted killer and was sentenced to death.

When Darkness Came Near

Has there ever been a safe time in human history? It seems from the beginning of time, the nature of man has made our world an unsafe place. But I felt growing up in the 1950s in the rural setting of Bucks County was a relatively secure place.

Until one day it wasn't...

We lived in a quiet neighborhood with humble homes separated by wooded lots. This was the age of the one car family. Dads were the bread-winners, and moms were the bread-makers. Moms stayed home to care for their home and family, and errands were usually carried out on foot. Remember, it was still the black and white time of *Ozzie and Harriet* and *Lassie*.

One day, shortly after I came home from school, my mother split up our errands. She went on ahead to the butcher, and I went in the opposite direction to Austin's farm for eggs and butter.

I was glad for the time alone so I could finally read the love sonnet passed to me in my seventh grade homeroom that afternoon. The treasured piece was safely tucked in my pocket.

Innocence walked along the hill among sparsely scattered houses. Loud, screeching brakes suddenly interrupted my deep distraction. Startled, I looked up to see a man jump out of his car, leaving the door wide open. With a brisk gait he came toward me with darkness in his eyes. I dropped the note and fled to the other side of the road to run toward home. He chased hard after me. I could hear heavy breathing sounds close behind.

Running, running faster, but I knew he was catching up to me. I wasn't sure if the pounding sounds I heard were my heart, his heavy steps, or the echo of my own racing across the stones.

A sharp pull on my hair yanked my head back and brought me down on one knee, grinding my leg into loose cinders. From the corner of my eye I could see dirty fingernails gripping my tangled hair. Somehow, I squirmed free. He grabbed me by the back of my blouse, shredding the seam.

I got away.

Blinded by fear and running with only one shoe, I could scarcely see in front of me. Blood mixed with gravel trickled down my leg. I ran into a neighbor's dirt driveway. The dogs were barking, and a wide-eyed Mrs. Dexter hurried to the door. Wiping her hands on her apron, she tried to brush the disheveled hair from my face.

"Verna, what is it? What's wrong?"

"I just need my mom. Have you seen her?"

"She just crossed the field a short time ago," she said. "Should I..."

In the middle of her sentence, I started across her backyard, through another, over the church field, finally out to the street where I was certain my mother must be by now.

Looking both ways, I crossed over the "main" road. There he was. Parked on the far right straddling a ditch, watching for me in the rearview mirror. He motioned with a slow, haunting wave.

Choking with fear, I ran inside the small market. The elderly shop owner looked over his bifocals. "What happened, kid? Did'ya fall off yer bike?"

"No...where's my mom?" I could barely be heard.

She had been there and left.

Trembling, I looked through the storefront window. He was gone.

I noticed a friend from school standing on the other side of the street. I ran out to him blurting, "Andy, will you go the long way home, past my house?"

"Sure. Are you okay?" He looked like he wanted to ask more.

I didn't say a word during the awkward journey. Finally, right before we got to my house, he asked again, "Are you sure you're okay?"

"I fell," I mumbled.

I was home.

Bolting through the screen door, I ran to my mother. She listened nervously as I explained what happened. After realizing I was safe, she said quietly, "Thank God."

I thought it was just a phrase.

She called the police. Our hometown, a little like Mayberry, had only one or two on the force. The officer came to the house, took the description of the man and the car, and wrote up a report.

My dad came home shortly after my mother cleaned up my bleeding leg. Anger and fear rushed over his countenance as I stuttered over my words. Color drained from his face as he looked at my torn and dirty clothing.

Sternly he muttered, "If you weren't wearing those tight shorts, it wouldn't have happened."

Innocent and gangly, I wasn't even thirteen years old yet, and I was a skinny ninety-four pounds.

The coarse remark made my heart sink further.

I wondered if he was right.

The newspaper worded the small article as "neighborhood girl molested." What did *molested* mean? Kids talked at the bus stop, naming possible names. Who was the girl? I was quiet.

I told no one about what happened except best friend, Rosemary. We looked for the car whenever we were outside and wondered if the man would come back.

Months passed, but the memory didn't. I rehearsed the scene over and over in my young mind. How did I get away? What if I didn't? What if it happens again?

Every afternoon I brought the newspaper in for my dad when he came home from work. Sometimes I'd glance at it while walking up to the door. But, on this day, different from anytime before, I stopped dead when I saw the picture and shocking headlines. The front page revealed a vaguely familiar face, vacant and cold eyes beneath creased brows. It described a horrific story about a man who brutally raped and killed a sixteen-year-old girl.

He was also suspected of two violent murders in nearby communities. Graphic headlines were rare in the age of innocence. I'd never read anything so ugly.

I stared. I got sick. Now his face was in black and white, but just as real.

He was the darkness that appeared in the light of day on an unforgettable afternoon, when God's hand was closer than his and protected me from the grope of hell.

26

It took years for me to realize my mother's words, "Thank God," were not just a familiar phrase. It took longer for me to realize I wasn't to blame for what happened that day when I recounted my father's words.

By grace I escaped.

He was the last person to receive death by the electric chair in the state of Pennsylvania in 1962.

Crumbs

Looking back over the hard-to-understand things that touch our lives, we realize it could only be a sovereign God watching over us. The realization that danger came so near in my young life became more apparent to me as an adult. For a long time I closed my mind to what happened...or what could have happened. A skinny young girl escaped the clutches of a predator. How?

The question remains. Why was I spared this harrowing experience but not the countless ones that followed? Also, why are there so many who are not spared terrible incidents? God's mysteries unanswered.

How grateful I am, Father, that You are the One whose holy eye is upon us even before our appointed birth. You have a biography already written for each one of Your children to carry out Your plan. It is only You I can praise for rescuing me on that day and for eternity because of Your Son, Jesus.

When have you experienced God's protection?

But the Lord is faithful,
and He will strengthen and protect you
from the evil one.

2 Thessalonians 3:3

What is broken when we break a sacred vow?
A heart, a family?
What are the lasting effects,
and how do we get beyond the hurt?

Covenant of Betrayal

An unwelcome stranger entered my house through an open window late one summer afternoon. The raspberry bush growing beneath the kitchen window was a perfect hiding place to crawl onto the ledge of the open window. Busy scrubbing the sink, I quickly turned when I heard a hollow thud behind me. A long black snake fell from the ledge onto the kitchen floor.

I screamed like a girl!

Barefoot, I stepped high across the cool linoleum to grab the broom to sweep it out the back door. The scaled intruder whipped across the floor and slithered under the refrigerator. *You're kidding.*

Realizing it was close to the time when my husband would be leaving from work, I thought I could catch him before he left on errands. Earlier in the day he'd reminded me he might be late. I leaped onto the kitchen counter and leaned far, fumbling for the phone, fixing my watchful eye on the snake's hiding place.

It's not easy to remember a phone number...or your name, while staring at an unseen snake.

Please, somebody pick up the phone!

The male voice on the other end said he would check if my husband was still in the building. It seemed to take forever. Waiting and definitely watching...

Finally, he spoke into the phone. "Sorry, you just missed them."

"Them?"

"Yeah, he just pulled away with his wife a few minutes ago," he said nonchalantly.

Disbelieving, I sank down onto the kitchen counter. Finally realizing what I just heard, I robotically shuffled back to the sink and finished scrubbing. I needed something to be clean. I felt as dead as the wilted wildflowers on the windowsill.

The snake no longer mattered.

This was the beginning and the end—the beginning of a series of betrayals, and the end of believing in people. Anyone.

My newlywed husband came home much later to a weeping wife, a barely listening wife, who soon became an enraged wife. The scent of pretension reeked with lying shouts that eventually confirmed he had a girlfriend he'd met at work.

I told him to leave and take the *other* serpent with him.

Reluctantly, I called my mom. "Tommy has a girlfriend," I blurted before she knew who was on the other end. Her anxious tone made things worse. I could overhear my dad in the background reminding me I had "made my bed, now lie in it." Slowly, I hung up in the middle of her sentence.

Nowhere to turn.

Seventeen, eight weeks pregnant, and married less

than four months, I was heading for divorce. I knew I was alone except for the one growing inside me. I didn't know God, I had no church, and no one for support except high school friends who were only thinking about high school. I felt isolated and cornered.

What do you do when life completely unravels soon after tying the knot?

Crumbs

A snake slithered among the crumbs of poor choices on my pathetic path. At seventeen I thought my life was over. I grew up fast and strong, but I couldn't catch up to the speed of my circumstances.

The symbolism of deceit fell at my feet on the day I learned of my husband's infidelity for the first time. The pattern of deception continued for the next twelve years. The road kept leading me to the same sorry starting place. The silent creeping serpent wraps around the one who sits near.

The truth was, the one I was listening to was a far greater deceiver than the one I married. The star of the cosmic drama that took place in Eden whispered over my life.

And, I listened.

Have you believed the lie that you are worthless?

"You are of your father the devil...
He was a murderer from the beginning,
and does not stand in the truth
because there is no truth in him.
Whenever he speaks a lie,
he speaks from his own nature,
for he is a liar and the father of lies."

John 8:44

Rescued by God's grace out of a desperate time of life,
I was left to raise three small children alone.
My Woodstock lifestyle turned into a dramatic conversion due to
my children attending a Christian school.

Abandoned Not Alone

I've made enough mistakes to know the choices we make—*make us*. And the choices others make can break us when we become part of their story.

Shortly after our daughter was born, my husband and I returned to the church where we were married to seek counseling. We wanted to stay together for her sake despite painful interruptions in our relationship. We thought it would get better.

After a fake reconciliation, we restated our "I do's" and didn't.

And couldn't.

There were reasons my husband was incapable of an "I do." His childhood scars were deep, and before long his scars became mine. We seem to inherit the issues of others when we step inside their story.

So, we played house for everyone. We bought a home on the edge of Philadelphia, and baby number two came for us. But baby number three came for him. Around the same time as our son's birth, I learned another child was just born to my husband.

Self-inflicted blindness helped me get through the sick cycle of breaks and repairs. He went to work. I stayed home and cared for babies, but our homelife spun out of control the more we became involved in music. Tommy was the lead singer and guitarist of a popular band, often the opening band for big names. It turned into an unhealthy environment that left too much of the outside—inside. Women became more of our problem. We lived in a glasshouse where everyone could see our scandal. I know at least a dozen people who could write this portion of my story—accurately. They knew more of what was going on in my life than I did.

A constant surge of band wannabes and strangers came in and out of our house day and night. Yet, the most unknown stranger was the one sharing the roof. Everything was changing. The glasshouse had a glass foundation doomed to crack wide open. I could only hope I'd fall out.

I met a lot of crazy people along the way, especially in my circle. They were a little different from his circle, but both equally damaging. We went separate ways together.

My June Cleaver image turned into Grace Slick. And then came a huge turn on the rocky uphill path we'd been traveling for years.

In spite of our unusual lifestyle, we agreed to send our children to a Christian school. *Why?* I was the furthest thing from a Christian. Ah, but there was a glitch. The requirement for entrance was that one parent had to be a "born-again" believer. My husband signed the paper.

Wow, I didn't want to be one.

I remember our first time attending a parent-teacher fellowship. We looked like an explosion from a freak show landing in the center of the conservative chosen. Beads on my hips, chains on his... He had more earrings than me. Did you ever feel like you didn't fit in? Did you make sure you didn't? That was me.

It didn't take long before a pastor affiliated with the school stopped by. Unannounced. Janis Joplin was screaming "Piece of My Heart" on the stereo. He asked me to turn down the loud music. Since there was a nude picture of her to cover a fist mark from a battle the night before, it was impossible to lift the damaged lid. The perplexed pastor tried to act as if he didn't see it and asked if he could pray with me. I said, "No, thanks."

The visit seemed longer than labor.

Short hemlines on daughter and long hairlines on son were reasons to bring along the prim schoolmarm who appeared stuffed and mounted in my living room, turning me even further away. I didn't know what I had gotten myself into and thought of putting them back into public school.

But in the middle of the madness, something happened to break the spell...or curse.

Something was stirring while listening to my children reciting their Scripture memory homework. And then... they asked if I would take them to the church associated with the school. Really? Who says no when your child asks you to take them to church?

I really didn't want to go. I didn't belong. But, I went... alone.

Meanwhile, things changed quickly when I became pregnant with our third child. Going through the same old pathetic cycle, I foolishly thought this new baby just might make the difference. It didn't.

The only thing that became different was me, when God leaned down to fix a broken child.

One September Sunday in 1975, while hiding between my children in the back pew, a holy shove unexpectedly picked me up and pushed me down the aisle. And *just as I am,* I went forward, dragging my darkness into the light. Joining the unborn child inside, a hallowed Resident came to live within me on this unforgettable day. Re-birth before birth—I was the one who was actually delivered first.

The huge crumb on my path that changed my life... forever.

But converted...now what?

I suddenly discovered there was something bigger than me...and my circumstances. I returned home on this life-altering day with the same problems waiting on the other side of the door. But now, I saw them differently. Now I had hope.

The first time I smelled the fresh pages of Scripture, I believed there might be a way to breathe in truth, but I didn't know how. I became a fickle church tramp and visited a new church every week but tried to avoid contact in hopes that no one could see my past from the good view down their nose. I couldn't see Jesus in the crowd. The judges and hypocrites were in the way. I had done so much wrong. I thought it showed.

I had no one to disciple me, no mentor, and no Christian friends or family. And my life was a mess. But I listened while my children read ancient stories of those in the Bible who were actually human and experienced changed lives because of Jesus. I listened to them recite their Scripture memory verses and heard for the first time that God could love even me.

Unknown at the time, I was months away from the calamity that changed my world. The One who knows all things, saw me alone raising three small children.

Baby boy was finally born, growing faster than me. I felt as newborn as the helpless one demanding to be nursed. In the distance I could hear the hissing of hell calling me back as I bowed lower. I didn't know how to go forward with this new thing that happened on that September Sunday. Do I make new friends, listen to different music...and God, what about this marriage? Am I supposed to fix it all?

It got fixed with more brokenness. When my baby turned six weeks old, my husband made his final exit. This time he wasn't involved with another woman. He was involved with our best friend's daughter.

Where was hope now?

On His way...

Crumbs

God found me in a dark pit of regrettable choices and used my children to bring me to Himself. They introduced me to the Creator, my re-Creator.

Coming out of a dark past is like emerging from a tunnel. We have to become acclimated to the Light. It was then I could see the crumbs that were worthy to gather.

I thought I had to make life changes in my own strength, like I had been taught as a child. I was wrong.

No matter our past, no matter our now...through the unexplained grace and power of Jesus we can be transformed into a new beginning.

Have you ever felt abandoned?

"Be strong and courageous,
do not be afraid or tremble at them,
for the Lord your God is the one who goes with you.
He will not fail or forsake you."

Deuteronomy 31:6

If we walk far enough
we shall sometime come to someplace.
Dorothy, The Wonderful Wizard of Oz

On the Road from Oz to Uz

What is true faith?

A friend's mother showed me what true faith looked like when I was a young girl. Later in life I met a few who showed me what it didn't look like. If I were to answer without looking it up, I would say true faith is believing God will do what He says He will do, trusting Him to be God, and waiting on His timing no matter how things look to our naked and very human eye.

I was twenty-nine years old when I came to the Lord...or when He came to me and rescued me out of a desperate time. I don't know what I expected. Maybe I was a little like Dorothy standing on the black and white before being transported to the colorized version of Oz complete with the gift of ruby red shoes. The bright new world over the rainbow where troubles melt like lemon drops...and you know the rest.

For a while, I thought when I asked for Oz, the Lord must've heard Uz and dropped me off on Job's side of town. "There was a man in the land of Uz whose name was Job" (Job 1:1).

39

We've all heard of the notorious example of tragedy...of the man who wasn't dealt the best deal. Even I had heard of him. Job was a real person who lived in a land south of Jordan. He suffered real pain. His was a story I was drawn to in the new Book I was reading.

Job was a wealthy man who lost everything, including his health and children. In his grief, he questioned why he had been born. But he refused to let a little loss or much loss get in the way of his relationship with his God. He continued to believe beyond belief. More about Job a little later.

Trials shook hard throughout my first year of meeting Jesus. He kept me close while the powers battled. It wasn't easy relinquishing my will into His custody.

I did my best raising my children alone, but it was difficult to understand what was going on in my life. I resented being reminded of my reality and continued to wear a daily mask of courage to shield my children from their reality. I was sure my self-reliance could see me through.

After a good cleaning out by the Holy Spirit, I began to grow. Circles of friends changed. I needed to move from old ties and stumbling blocks, but I wasn't sure how.

And then, another rescuer came into my life... Surprisingly, I came across an old acquaintance who knew me when I was living in my glasshouse.

"I heard through the grapevine you've had a rough time," Jeff said shyly, while all six feet three inches of him looked down into my broken eyes.

Hmm, for once the grapevine was accurate about me. After I shared an abbreviated version of what happened, he asked if "all of us" would like to go to dinner. And so, our first date was an intimate dinner for five.

The following year we were married. We relocated nearly forty miles away. Life, I was certain, would be good in a new land. No one walks down the aisle, especially a second time, and thinks things will get worse...but in many ways they did.

Our first year together I wondered if hell burst open and spilled out onto my roof. My child nearly died of a rare condition. I suffered a miscarriage while caring for my terminally ill father. My new husband lost his business. Two close friends died a few months apart. All within twelve months. The past twelve years had been hard in a difficult marriage, but now for all of this to be condensed into twelve months...

What else could happen?

Throughout our married life, now going on thirty-eight years, we have had a collection of messes and miracles. After all, he brought his suitcase and I brought mine, and then our together junk poured out all over life.

Many have asked, "Why did you stay with God? How did you stay with God? How much can one family endure?"

And my favorite, "Do you think you're cursed?"

I understand well-meaning friends that question the intensity and recurrence of so many trials coming to our family. I've had a few questions of my own, especially when being referred to as Job-ette, which I absolutely hate. And I've asked, "Where were You, Father, when I was going through the pain of divorce, prodigals, prison, comas, and transplants?"

Right there. He never moved.

While going through his crisis of faith, Job met up with a few fair-weather friends who comforted him with the good counsel that it may have been his sin that caused his calamity. Despite friends who prodded him to blame God, or a wife who advised him to curse God, he never abandoned his belief. Why do you think that is? Because he had true faith—the kind that doesn't deny or bail when things go wrong.

Job trusted God. God trusted Job.

His answer to his friends, "Though He slay me, I will hope in Him" (Job 13:15). He argued with God from time to time, but he soon found out when God speaks the debate is over.

If Job and I could sit down and trade war stories, he would definitely win, but I think he would kindly say, "'He knows the way I take. When he has tried me, I shall come forth as gold. My foot has held fast to His path; I have kept His way and not turned aside' (Job 23:10–11). And you understand this path, Verna."

Dorothy got swept up to the Land of Oz by a cyclone... but it didn't lead home.

Crumbs

In the classic story of The Wonderful Wizard of Oz, *we see Dorothy, after an exhausting trip along the yellow brick road, standing before an invisible man behind the curtain. The one she believed would get her safely home.*

I've gathered countless crumbs, some too big to carry, along the path from Oz to Uz. But I've discovered God is not the unavailable power behind the veil but the all-knowing Father who permits the things in our life to lead us closer into His presence.

What has God used along your journey
to lead you home?

You will show me the path of life;
In Your presence is fullness of joy.
Psalm 16:11 NKJV

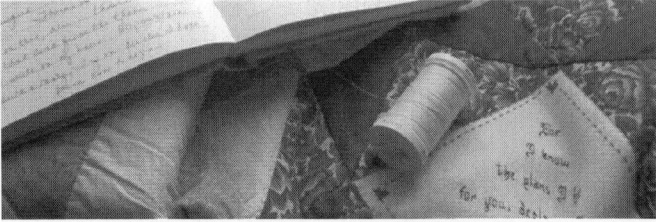

Faith is believing in things
when common sense tells you not to.

George Seaton

After his father died, an unwanted child
was raised in a Philadelphia orphanage.
He knew how it felt to be abandoned.
God used him to rescue an abandoned family—
and used the family to rescue him.

Chosen Orphan

Young Jeff stood at the side of an open field watching a tractor cut the earth. He couldn't believe his eyes when the harrow split wide open a too-slow turtle. The angry boy chased after the tractor and yelled up to the farmworker, "You're mean!"

He scowled down and laughed.

Jeff picked up as big a clump of dirt as his small hands could hold to thrust at the tractor wheel. Abruptly, the engine came to an idle. The irate driver jumped down, grabbed the boy, and tied him spread-eagle to the side of the huge rear wheel. He drove off recklessly through deep ditches—the cruel punishment for a five-year-old, heartbroken over a turtle.

Another common discipline Jeff experienced was to get locked overnight in a dark chicken coop to protect the hens from predators. But there was no one to protect the frightened child from this kind of mistreatment.

Buried memories don't die.

Jeff found out too young that parents die, when one snowy December morning his father was taken away on a horse-drawn sled. He watched from the window as the image faded into the West Virginia holler. It was the week before Christmas when he saw his dad for the last time. Before his mid-January birthday, his mother sent him and his younger brother to a small Pittsburgh shelter for unwanted children. He remained there for two years.

When Jeff was just seven years old, he was placed on an overnight train to Philadelphia. Destination—Girard College, an orphanage for poor and fatherless boys. His only belongings were what he was wearing and a note pinned inside his jacket to identify him to the governess meeting him at the station.

With the exception of a few trips to visit his aunt and her family in western Pennsylvania, Jeff remained enclosed within high stone walls until he was nearly eighteen. He was lonely and disappointed when he was unable to go to the farm to visit his cousins. The only hope was when a family came during the holidays to temporarily adopt one of the boys. Jeff grew fast and tall, so he was often overlooked. The older orphans were chosen after the little guys were picked. He remembers one Christmas when out of twelve hundred Girard boys, only eight were left behind.

He was one of them.

Jeff doesn't talk much about his childhood, but as a mom, I know there was no one to tuck him in at night, no bedtime stories, no kiss and a Band-Aid to fix a split knee. So, through the years, he learned to fend for himself.

When it was time to leave the stone cocoon, he left with the clothing he was wearing. Jeff was grateful for the education and his ninety brothers of Girard, but...

It seemed there was always a *but,* a *what if,* or an *I wish...*

Destination—world. Now what?

He joined the Marines. Married, divorced. Married again, divorced again. Finally, at thirty-nine years old, for the first time he became part of a family when he married into our instant one. He came along at a fragile time in our lives, and we in turn made the difference in his.

It was a big decision to take on the responsibility of a pre-teen daughter, a nine-year-old son who missed his dad terribly, and a fourteen-month-old baby. Jeff didn't have a father that he could remember, and he hadn't experienced being a father, so it was quite a challenge to meet their various emotional needs. Each one had felt the rejection of when a parent leaves the home. Growing up with his (unrelated) Girard brothers helped Jeff learn the importance of being a family—one family. When our son was born, he did not show favoritism or consider us a blended family. Just one.

Crumbs

It reminds me of how our good Father chooses us and grafts us into His large family. No favorites—no stepchildren. We are given the right to be His children by receiving and believing in Jesus.

At times many of us feel unclaimed or overlooked. We see our circumstances through orphan-eyes and forget it was God's plan before creation to adopt us. The pictures we find hard to omit from childhood can become painted with grace the moment we enter the family of God as His chosen orphans.

We can choose to be chosen—will you?

See what great love the Father has lavished on us,
that we should be called children of God!
And that is what we are!
1 John 3:1 NIV

Reputations can always be reversed.
God, the name changer, gave me a new name
and removed the identity I gave myself.

Renamed

"Is that Verna Rose?" someone whispered. "Isn't she the one...?"

Have you ever noticed how gossip feeds a reputation so well it becomes too heavy to carry? It's strange—a guy gets into a fight when he's young and gets the reputation for being a bully. It doesn't necessarily mean he was a bully. It may just mean he was in a fight. But, somehow, it's remembered, and his reputation seems to travel with him for life.

I had a bad reputation in school. I was in school a *long time ago*, and yet people I haven't seen for decades continue to remember the wild, argumentative girl of yesteryear. Peers started rumors others believed, and passed on...and on.

I remained angry for many years, making it difficult for anyone to come near, including God. I tried to make myself even more unlikable.

After my life took a dramatic shift, I loved reading the examples in the Bible of miraculously changed lives. But even from those accounts, what do we remember most?

Look at Mary Magdalene. This poor woman has stayed bad for two thousand years due to misinterpretation. She was Mary of Magdala, like Saul of Tarsus, Jesus of Nazareth…or maybe, Verna of Bensalem. Whisper down the lane has made her a prostitute, but actually she was possessed by seven demons cast out by Jesus. Some try and identify her as a couple other Marys in the Scriptures, but there isn't a scrap of evidence that she was a prostitute…just a cleansed lady. Check out her story in Luke 16. It tells of a godly woman with a negative past.

Since I am remembered for a dark past, it gives me hope knowing that someone with seven devils could someday be a saint. Because of Jesus.

When I was young, I loved fixing broken dolls and patching up the wounded. A quick fix, stitching on a shoe-button eye or repairing a hole in the knee, made the doll look new. So, I renamed her.

My mistakes renamed me. In my mid-teens, I felt like one of the broken, in desperate need of repair. Issues and anger can break us wide open at the seams. It didn't help that I was the only one in school with an unusual name that didn't seem to need a last one, sort of like Cher. I couldn't hide behind the Ann's and the Sue's…

Rock throwers reminded everyone I had tarnished my name. Later, I became my own rock thrower, looking in the rearview mirror and seeing every wrong thing in my background.

We've heard *what's done is done*, but Jesus says what's done can be cast out and erased. It took me some time to learn forgiveness is the gift we give ourselves. It comes with the fragrant offering of a new name, inscribed on His hand.

I think of those in the Bible who God renamed when He gave them a new story. Abraham, Jacob, Paul, and Peter. My last name has changed a few times, and with it so has my story. But my old name, Verna, is my new name...and I like my new name. It means *spring*, rebirth.

No matter what we've done or who we've been, Christ repairs the tatters and the wounds. He makes us brand new. Renamed. The only One whose reputation cannot change is Jehovah God, the Eternal-unchangeable.

Crumbs

When your name becomes your shame, God can give you a new one. The crumbs I was gathering along my journey of brokenness were shame and distrust. Shame is a painful emotion. When we carry shame, we reject ourselves and expect others to do the same. Including God. But this is what the mouth of the Lord says,

> **You shall be called by a new name,**
> **which the mouth of the LORD will name.**
> **You shall also be a crown of glory**
> **In the hand of the LORD.**
> Isaiah 62:2–3 NKJV

I am named by God. So are you.

Has your shame renamed you? Don't let it.

> **Neither be disgraced,**
> **for you will not be put to shame;**
> **For you will forget the shame of your youth.**
> Isaiah 54:4 NKJV

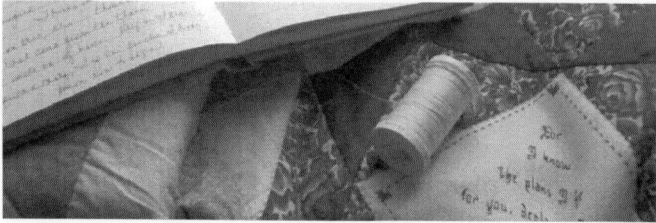

My story may look like one of despair,
but it is one of grace and rescue.
God is not a God of despair
but a God of restoration.

The story of a faithful daughter,
the thread of hope holding me together
when I felt most frayed.

Daughter Thread of Hope

Full with descending infant and a butter-smeared afternoon snack, my water unexpectedly broke. It's always unexpected, even after waiting nine months. I went into labor with my first child in the far-off land before cell phones. I couldn't reach my husband, so I called my parents to take me to the hospital.

Hours later, a baby girl was painfully delivered and scrubbed pure pink when my husband finally arrived. She was miraculously helpless. I couldn't know then I'd turn around to see her grown.

When it was time to be discharged, my husband and parents drove together to bring us home. Strained joy and silence made the ride home more of a labor than the one on the way there. It became obvious the tension between them was due to the reason my husband was unavailable for most of the blessed event.

It wasn't the homecoming I planned.

I sensed what was ahead. I wanted to wrap her in a swaddling prayer. But I didn't know how.

Somehow baby girl got me through this portion of life.

She spoke hope to me before she could utter a word. The sweet bundle depending on a teenage girl to raise her was a challenging new beginning...for both of us. She was the thread holding life together in a tattered marriage. A huge responsibility for a newborn, I think.

Then...

Wiser than a toddler has a right to be, she climbed up my thighs and reached right into my heart. Every inch she grew made me bigger.

Wiser than a child has a right to be, at nine years old, she announced her desire to become a missionary. The little girl with rawhide woven into shiny auburn braids dug deep in the hard moments to find something deeper. She showed me God.

Wiser than a teen has a right to be, she taught me to trust. It was then, I realized, I delivered my best friend.

Wiser than a young woman has a right to be, after graduating high school, she followed her missionary dream and later married her high school sweetheart. Her little-girl goal showed me life could turn out the way we hope...the way we dream.

She'd scarcely put her toys away when the ballet-dancing, brownie-badge-collecting, cheerleading, cross-stitching, secret-sharing mini-me had become larger than life.

Then, in the blink of a tear, she was a bride clothed in white grace. Another blink, and...Mama to mama, I watched her bend low over her own hope-threads in a cradle.

When my heart had enough and I didn't know where to turn, I had the daughter the Father breathed into me at a young age. She was thread mending a ripped life.

In the dark times when I questioned if I failed, she

proved I hadn't. She chose well, married well, and raised her children well. She is the one who continues to remind me God's grace paints over our choices with glory to make them beautiful.

I admire the lady.

**"Many daughters have done nobly,
But you excel them all."**
Proverbs 31:29

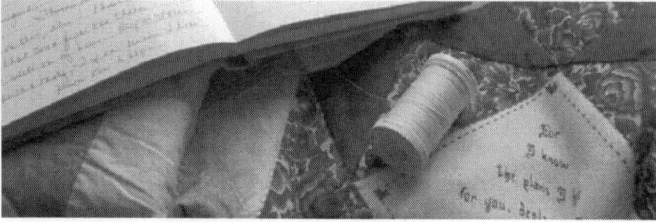

It's easier to believe than to explain why..

"Are not two sparrows sold for a cent?
And yet not one of them will fall to the ground
apart from your Father."
Matthew 10:29

When Sparrows Fall

When sparrows fall, does it mean that God looked away for the moment? I remember the day and the hour that I found the answer.

No, it wasn't on the life-changing day when I came to Jesus. It was on the me-changing day a few years later when I came to *know* Him.

During the short time from when I first became a believer until the birth of my last child, I experienced more turmoil in my life than ever before.

Yet, I didn't know how to pray or believe for God-sized answers until something devastatingly beautiful took me to a deeper place. Face-to-face, eye-to-eye with the absurdity of life without really knowing God.

I shouted at, and wrestled with, the Father who allowed my child to be born on a day he wasn't due—in a way I never wanted—for a purpose too sacred to speak.

Of course, he was *due*. He arrived in an ordained instant.

Life seemed to leave my body when they took him from my womb, even worse, when they took him from the hospital. Babies should come with a warning label that reads *this baby will change your life.*

What just happened?

Doctors wouldn't tell me. My husband couldn't tell me. The first-time-father was racing the helicopter to a Philadelphia hospital to find out. What. Just. Happened.

All I could do was wait.

A blank stare at the pages of my open Bible saw nothing but white space. It was like trying to find a picture on a blank canvas. I looked out the window to check if the stars and moon were still in their place. They shouldn't have been. Nothing was.

In the night when life is dark, we learn to pray.

In the night when hungry infants are brought to mamas who are waiting to nurse them full, no one came to my room.

At daybreak, I remember being grateful when I heard commotion in the corridor drowning out the sound of a crying baby. A stern-faced nurse wheeled a disheveled teenage girl into my room. She sat quietly. Her silence told me she was desperate, like me.

The hushed whispers in the hallway told me about her. The scared girl had attempted to deliver her baby in the bushes outside of the hospital. An employee coming on shift at the same time saw what was happening.

She must have been as desperate to discard her baby as I was to keep mine.

God's eye was on the rescued newborn, but I wondered if His eyesight was sharp enough to see my child so far away. Having her in the same room only added to my despair. My postpartum blues were getting discolored. The color of grief comes in black if we choose to wear it, but there was *nothing* left in my closet.

Gazing out the window, I breathed a feeble prayer for two little lives.

I saw a bird die in flight.

Ordinarily, I may have considered the disturbing sight as some kind of twisted omen. Instead, I was reminded in that moment, how the Father's eye was watching over a baby about to be abandoned, a baby fighting for life in an inner city hospital, and a sparrow falling to earth.

This was the hard and loving lesson in learning to surrender to His will. If my son didn't live, it didn't mean that God looked away. It simply meant that I needed to keep my eyes fixed on His goodness, even when I blink.

Crumbs

Nothing is insignificant or of little value. Not sparrows, two for a penny, or the lives of His children worth every drop of His blood.

Our son is celebrating another birthday today. So are we.

Have you believed you are hidden from God's sight?

**The eye of the Lord is on those who fear Him,
on those who hope for His loving kindness
to deliver their soul from death.**
Psalm 33:18

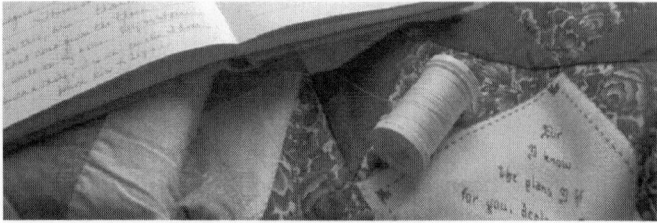

Faith is like stepping onto
an invisible bridge
and knowing it will get us
to the other side of our story.

*Our youngest son was born with no kidney function
and transferred at birth to an inner-city hospital.
Unable to be with him due to the aftermath of his birth,
out of desperation I called a church in Philadelphia.
In spite of a paralyzing snowstorm,
a loving priest made the journey in my place.*

The Hallowed Surrogate

Complications from the emergency delivery prevented me from traveling to the distant hospital where my baby son was transported hours after being cut from his lifeline.

Left alone with an empty womb, I remained in the hospital for over a week.

When I finally returned home, it was more difficult to face our children waiting expectantly for their new brother than it was to face the sentence of bed rest. Hemorrhaging and transfusions left me no choice but to cooperate.

Only a prayer connected me to my baby I hadn't embraced yet. Haunted by a cry nearly forty miles away on a silent night kept me sound awake.

Who can out-watch the stars? I must have while keeping a nocturnal vigil in his little room. I wept over an empty cradle filled with gifts and no child. I listened in the darkness, imagining his baby breaths. Night was blacker than dark. Glazed streets separated houses put to sleep by the moon. Snow tumbled from heaven, making the roads impassable.

In the still of night. No one awake but God...and me. Watching together.

The faithful chime of the clock reminded me one more hour had passed for my infant son to be without me. I felt paralyzed. I couldn't drive, and I couldn't be driven. I thought I'd go mad if I couldn't get to him.

With only the faint glow of a book light, I fumbled recklessly through my Bible to find any answer to anesthetize me. The black letters strung together may as well have been invisible. Through swollen eyes, I stared through blank pages to the vacant crib across the room.

Finally, I came across a passage in Revelation, the divine ending. Being a faith rookie, nothing sounded comforting amidst stories of destruction and wars. I thought I must be in the wrong place, until I read the letter written to the angel of the church in Philadelphia. I had to be taking things out of context and geography.

But I heard Him...

For some reason I knew I was supposed to be right where I was. I waited for dawn to shake my husband awake. How could he even sleep? When I got a stir out of him, I asked, "What is the name of the church in Philadelphia that was on the news last night? Remember, it was about a miracle?"

Scarcely able, he muttered, "The Church of St. Peter and Paul, why?"

"I don't know, but I'm going to call there as soon as it's light."

I looked up the phone number and called the rectory. A soft-spoken man answered on the first ring. He somehow made sense of my rambling.

"My baby was flown to St. Christopher's Hospital. He's not expected to live," I blurted, choking on leftover tears.

He asked a few questions that I didn't know how to answer. Finally, I said, "I'm not of your faith. Will you help me?"

In perfect monotone sacristy, he replied, "Yes, my child, I will."

Jesus is non-denominational.

Later that morning, in spite of an impacted wisdom tooth, Father O'Toole walked fourteen blocks battling a blizzard that shut down the entire city and public transportation.

I pictured him. He must look like Bing Crosby in *Going My Way*. Black hem draping over snow-white mounds, making a hallowed trek at the same time I was clinging to the sacred hem of Jesus. Believing.

The nurse called. She told me how the priest searched empty corridors to find my child, and how he bent low to hum a prayer over the fragile infant plugged into technology.

We were told we would have to be trained to dialyze our baby at home. Three hours after Father O'Toole left our baby's side, he was weaned from the machine. Three months later, he came home to us. Thirteen years later, our son finally needed a kidney transplant. We were grateful I could donate my kidney and be used in his healing.

After the surgery, we called the parish to contact the loving surrogate who went in my place thirteen years before and tell him the good news. Sadly, we were informed Father O'Toole was very sick and had been transferred to a home for aging priests. Our son, Geoff, wanted to write him a note.

Two weeks before Father O'Toole passed away he received a note from the little boy he'd prayed for so long ago. Holding the letter with trembling hand, close to his failing eyes, he read:

> You probably won't remember me. I was the baby that you came to visit and pray for many years ago. My mom told me that you had an impacted wisdom tooth and walked fourteen blocks in a snowstorm.
>
> I wanted to let you know God heard you and healed me, but when I called to let you know, I heard you were very sick. Now it's my turn to pray for you.
>
> Love Geoff

Gazing out of the nursing home window with a faint smile of remembrance, the humble priest nodded, revisiting the distant moment. I doubt if he expected his charitable deed on that wintry day to one day be recorded in a book.

This story was written the day before our son's thirty-third birthday. Although the sun was shining on the day I was writing, I recall clearly the blizzard of '79. I won't forget the love of God, dressed like man wearing priestly garments, who made the sacrificial journey in my place.

I never will.

Crumbs

I wasn't familiar with the stories in the Bible that told of miracles, but somehow I believed for one for my son. When blizzards and bleeding kept me apart from my newborn, this treasured crumb in my collection of blessings was instrumental in changing my life forever.

This is the time on my path when God began to grow my faith in a new dimension, and I met Him in a way that has never left me.

What has God used in your life in a dramatic way?

For nothing will be impossible with God.
Luke 1:37

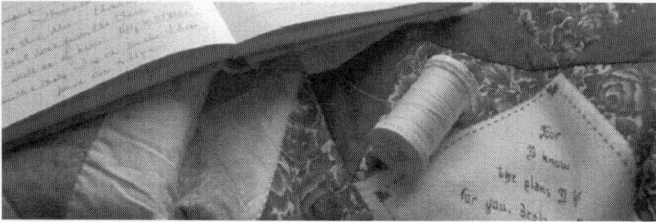

When we can't hear His voice,
may we listen for His breath.

Blocks of life pieced together create an heirloom,
that for such a time as this I was here.
And so was He.

Stitches and Stones

Has the journey of your life led to where you once thought it would take you? We may get there, but for most of us, it's not without the hurdles and detours.

When I was in grade school, the teacher asked the class a fairly simple question, "What would you like to be when you grow up?" I should have just said "happy" and left it at that.

Since my last name began with "R," I had a multiple choice to mimic by the time it was my turn. But the string of teacher, nurse, astronaut, and president wannabes didn't impress me. Finally. Mrs. Pickerskill (and yes, that was her name) looked down from under her bun and over her bifocals to wait for my answer. "A wife and a mom," I said confidently. All eyes were on me while waiting for the finish.

"Uh, that's about it," was the only ending I could come up with. I guess it sounded less motivated than the high ambition of the others, even back in the Donna Reed days of the 1950s. After all, she was the ultimate heels-and-pearls housewife who made everything run like clockwork. I liked her.

I reached my goal prematurely and became a wife and mom sooner than most.

I wasn't experienced in a thing, but here's a little in how I got my degree...

I didn't know how to cook. I ruined eggs. My new husband patiently showed me a few things to help us survive, but I wanted to do more than just stay alive. So, the thing to do was to enroll in a home economics class at the local high school and learn some basics.

It didn't start off well. I instantly got a thumbs-down on the bread project when the instructor had to chip away the crust to dig out the white stuff. Who knew yeast could be so important? After getting the hang of it, I wanted more than just basics, so I went on to gourmet classes. After perseverance and practice, I not only learned to cook, but actually became experienced enough to cater events.

I read every pink and blue book I could find on parenting as soon as I experienced morning sickness. It didn't take long to learn parenting skills weren't found in a manual. Having a child grows up a child. The more children I had, the more experienced I became—without the book.

Among countless inabilities on my *wash* bucket list to accomplish was sewing. Another failure. This time, a simple blouse. Apparently, it wasn't simple enough because I attached the sleeve into the neck seam. I remembered the bread incident and thought sewing couldn't be any worse than learning to cook. So, I went to the library and checked out a how-to book complete with pictures. I read the *Singer Basic Sewing* book from cover to cover, sat down with scissors and scraps, and created a layette for baby girl. After mastering the basics, I went on to tailoring classes. I not only learned to sew, but years later created a wedding dress for her. *Can you believe it?* So, the wife-mom thing was beginning to turn out well. I seemed to be a natural homemaker content with keeping house, sewing school clothes, and looking forward to laundry day. *Really.*

But life changed. Dramatically.

Having a husband in a band booked a few nights a week and every weekend, changed the dynamics of our family...and me. The more he became involved in things outside of marriage, the more curious I became to do the same, and before long the wild child began to resurface. I started a small sewing business, *Freak Froxx*, creating stage wear for performers, primarily rock bands. This dark shredded piece of life took me to places and people that surpassed the basics. It turned out to be a crash course in how to enter a pit and keep from being buried alive.

You'll have to read between the lines while I fast-forward from the "bad old days" to when an unexpected God brushed up against me. I could almost hear a holy hum while He worked overtime to get my attention. Then one day I turned and asked, "Who's there?" I didn't find out until my children told me.

Life changed. Again, dramatically.

Still fast-forwarding since some of this is in other stories. After a new husband, new location, and new direction in life, my career of designing freaky frocks ended and turned into a rather tame cottage industry creating primitive folk art dolls. What a contrast! My new business was sweetly named *Homespun Heritage.*

Did I mention I also loved to write? So, while on the way home from a Christian writers' conference in

Downingtown, I decided to combine my love of sewing and writing. The conference director, Marlene Bagnull, had no idea of the inspiration she would be in polishing a hidden gift.

The *Homespun Heritage* years were very different from my *Freak Froxx* season.

I created primitives to meet a popular market, but with a personal twist to reflect personalities of special people in my life. I attached a story card to each one. The first doll I designed was Martha Pickerskill, an old school-marm complete with spectacles and a *McGuffy's Reader*. You guessed it, my third grade teacher from the two-room schoolhouse who grilled me about future goals.

Unsatisfied with simply sewing, I wanted to learn to quilt. Admiring the extraordinary quilts made by the Amish in nearby Lancaster County, I wondered if I could learn the art of quilt making without being Amish.

So, I gave it a try. I began with a mess of small patches to make a quilt for my daughter to take along to the mission field. Precious scraps from her brownie uniform, flannel nightie, and first-day-of-school dress covered her with pieces of home while she was away. In spite of the visible mistakes, it was a masterpiece to her.

Remember, I'm not content with basics, so the next step was to join an advanced quilting course where I learned to construct a biblical sampler quilt. Each square represents a story in scripture, including favorites *Jacob's Ladder / Job's Tears*. This quilt would have to be my best-loved.

But it wasn't.

I began to journal when our fourth child was born with chronic kidney failure.

Recording the promises from God's Word kept me

going through difficult times, especially when my son was to receive his first transplant. Somehow, journaling helped make sense out of something so senseless.

After thirteen long years of preserving my journals in a dark drawer, my daughter and I decided to stitch the life-sustaining verses on fabric as a keepsake for our family. From first baby breath moment through years of the heart-pressing transplant journey, thread-engraved passages came to life.

The testimony quilt, written with needle and thread, not only tells the legacy of a Father's love woven within our child's illness but also traces a path of my personal faith journey. More than a quilt, it is a cherished record of sacred milestones of life.

My faith story begins in the same way everything else had. With basics. Maybe you're there right now. Holding onto crumbs—the small portion that says, *I know He can, but I don't know if He will.* God doesn't want us to settle for crumbs. By remaining in His Word, our small faith can grow into a tenacious faith that says, *I know He can, and I know He will.*

I believe the Father wants all of His children to know He can and He will.

Our life-stories can be told in a quilt. The front appears perfect for everyone to see, comfortable and tidy, the way we hope things seem to others. The backing is empty, like our lives without the Word. The batting in the middle covers our mess of tangles and failures, and the knots of trials create and hold tight the beauty of our faith.

My testimony quilt is an offering. Building altars in the desert was something the Israelites did while wandering from Egypt to the Promised Land when they experienced the greatness of God. They built altars of thanksgiving for His faithfulness. That's what I wanted to do. Every promise etched into a fabric square is a stone-reminder of the turning point in my life when God the Healer came down in a relentless way to shift my crooked path.

An altar set in place, that He visited my life for such a time as this, when I was here...and so was He.

Crumbs

I have come a long way from the third grade little girl with the simple goal, and the young woman who didn't know how to carry it out. How about you? Can you look back on your path and see the small crumbs that were easy to ignore, and the huge crumbs that weren't?

Remember, God doesn't want us to settle for basic crumbs. He wants to bless us with the larger portion.

The one thing that helps me to have courage to keep moving forward when I am at a crossroad, is to look at the altars I have built in the desert.

Do you have a rock of remembrance?

"Record the vision...
for the vision is yet for the appointed time;
It hastens toward the goal and it will not fail.
Though it tarries, wait for it;
For it will certainly come, it will not delay."
Habakkuk 2:2–3

Vultures on the path could no longer devour
the scattered bread of life
once I began to gather them as keepsakes.

When Crumbs Become Keepsakes

As far back as I can remember, my mom wore a marquesite ring on her left hand next to her wedding band. With its countless glittering stones, I thought it must have been more expensive than her simple diamond—especially since she always took it off when she washed the dishes. I can still see the time a shaft of sunlight hit the windowsill in such a way the reflection from the ring danced circles through the kitchen. I looked up wide-eyed and said, "Gee, Mom, that ring must have cost billions."

I loved her answer. "Most people would think it's of little value, but to me, it's priceless because it came at a dear cost."

She received the ring when she lost her mother.

I think back to when I considered things I received from the Father to be of little value—when I overlooked the tiny jewels because I was searching for a diamond.

Until a few years ago, I pretty much believed the Lord showed up in my life one huge time. How could I have thought that the life-changing September day in 1975, simply because I answered an altar call, was the first time? It wasn't until I started tearing through old journals and writing this book that I actually read my own story. Retracing my steps, it was plain to see the treasures left in litter.

Obviously, the first time was not the first time. He was just waiting outside.

The first time may have been when the Father was listening in on a childhood prayer. Now I lay me down to sleep...I pray my dad will stop drinking.

When he did, I thought it must be a coincidence.

Maybe another first time was when He was outside-inside the little Methodist church on the hill, lending His ear as I sang an old hymn. "Trust and obey...for there's no other way..." Surely, He knew I was there only because a neighborhood parent dropped a few of us kids off on a Sunday morning. I think He must've sat right down in the pew between mom and me when we stopped by on Easter Sunday.

I'm sure it grieved His heart that He had to wait a year to sit down with us again.

But the real first time must have been when I was twelve years old, chasing after a God I didn't know to ask if He could heal a dying classmate. After three weeks of praying hard and answered prayer, I left the crumbs in bicycle tracks.

How many firsts could there be? It had to be the one when the pastor of a local church was assigned as my husband's advisor. How could we not go to his church? It didn't mean much more to me than a place for marriage counseling and to have my new babies christened. Babies seemed to come with a christening requirement.

What meant nothing at the time is like found gold to me now because I see the importance of what was left in the dust. While Father God was looking in on me, I thought time and rebellion could cover His eyes. But it only covered mine.

Sort of like the two disciples on the road to Emmaus, we walk side-by-side brushing up against the Holy, not realizing until farther down the road whose imprints were beside ours. Then, something happens and our eyes are opened for the first time to the One who had been there all along standing outside waiting to come into our lives.

Thankfully, the door was left ajar when I enrolled my children in a Christian school. This is the milestone when the course of life changed radically, and I began following the One who had left pieces of Himself all over the path. *But how to begin?*

To begin with, I figured I needed a Bible to get to know Him a little better. Honestly, it wasn't something that came naturally. The first time I sat down with the Good Book, I kept tripping over the thee-thou-shall-nots, totally missing out on the love letter.

My approach had to be raw and juvenile if I would get anywhere with this. I started out with the children's version that my kids were reading, complete with cartoons and speech balloons. At least I got to know the cast in the animated story of Noah, Abraham, Jacob, Moses, David, and Paul, all pointing to the main character—Jesus.

I found out He was dying to meet me.

As a new Christian, I had a deep desire to know Him well. I s-l-o-w-l-y progressed to the *Living Bible*, a paraphrase that has a simple way of telling a simple message. I got it, but needed to dig deeper. So, I joined a few neighborhood Bible studies that weren't too threatening. You may remember from a few other stories I didn't do well in Christian circles at the time.

Farther on down the road, I joined a bunch of Jesus-lovin' gals who met on a Thursday morning at something called Precept. The inductive method of studying the Bible precept upon precept seemed somewhat intimidating. So, I started out with *Lord, I Want to Know You* followed by *Lord, Heal My Hurts.* Tears with words can only express what a difference this made in my life. I've continued for over twenty-five years to make Thursday morning Precept class my priority, and it's still making a difference in my life. It's been a compass to keep me on track. Only the Holy Spirit of God can take a redeemed rebel from speech balloons to Greek word studies, don't you think?

Like my mom's keepsake, some may see it as little value, but to me, it's priceless because it came with a dear cost.

Crumbs

Crumbs once tossed to the birds along the broken road became precious keepsakes. They were jewels of grace that nothing could replace or remove, the Word of God.

What are the keepsakes in your story?

Your word have I treasured in my heart.
Psalm 119:11

After relocating nearly forty miles away from home,
I found a new family. God provided sheltering friends
to help me find what was promised.

With a Little Help from My Friends

As of this moment, I've been on several different paths for 34,857 days. We can calculate the days, but not the number of people who have crossed our paths. It's strange how we meet so many people along the way and yet become close to only a handful.

During my many days of existence, things have changed in the way we interact with one another. We've become an impersonal society, chatting electronically instead of face-to-face. There was a time when neighbors chatted over the fence and dropped by to borrow sugar— kind of like Lucy and Ethel.

I wasn't one of them. I wasn't one for chatting over the fence. I avoided not only my neighbors, but people in general. Many heard me say, "You leave me alone, and I'll leave you alone." Except for a few close childhood friends, I found it hard to trust people.

It took time for me to learn that people are one of the very things that God uses in our lives. I think of what my life would be without the holy connections on my path. If we take a tour of our hearts to remember those who left tracks or caused cracks, we can see the good, bad, and even the ugly were used by design.

Even though Jesus had a few beloved friends walking the same dirt road, He also had a few who let Him down. They snoozed, ran away, and ratted Him out. But the Father used them to carry out His perfect plan.

We're going to meet all kinds of people who make up our stories. Those who betray, bewilder, and break, and those who embrace, encourage, and edify. Think of how the good and the bad played out in your life.

I see clearly how God's networking turned my life around, upside down, and took me to a place where I met people I didn't even know existed on my planet. Everything changed after 1975. I was reborn, remarried, relocated, and re-formed within a few short years. When my children and I started attending a church in Bucks County, we became acquainted with a new kind of people.

Within the first difficult months of married life in a new area, I definitely needed a new kind of people. Those who genuinely cared. Our family was turned inside out the first year of moving to Chalfont. It was a huge transition, especially for my children who experienced the trauma of divorce, losing a beloved grandparent, and getting a new everything—father, home, friends, and school. They were spinning, also.

Needless to say, we were grateful for the godly people of this church who were there to encourage new believers through the difficult times.

The following year, we moved again, this time to a farmhouse in Montgomery County. Life changed even more dramatically. After searching for a new church, we became disappointed in the one we found and knew we needed to move on.

One snowy Super Bowl night, I went to a Praise and Prayer meeting at Immanuel Leidy's Church. Since it was Super Bowl, every man was behind a television and there were only women there. Three. But there was something very present, very special, in this place. I couldn't wait to come back the following week to attend a worship service.

I found home.

I found family.

I found God.

It was easy to become part of the congregation. Our teenagers and toddlers fit in perfectly. Soon, the whole family became involved...serving and growing in faith.

I thought our first year of relocation was the difficult one, but it was simply a stepping-stone to the next level. Our Leidy's family was the heart, hands, and feet that the Lord used to carry us through years of painful circumstances. Every prayer and supporting kindness gave us the strength to take another step forward.

I think of the difficult journey of illness, hardship, lost jobs, lost home, and so much more that we didn't walk through alone because of God's unrelenting provision. All because over thirty years ago, I went to a Praise and Prayer meeting at a small church in Souderton on Super Bowl Sunday when hardly anyone was there...

...*but God.*

Crumbs

The greatest thing the Lord has done for me is to make me part of His Body, for the common bond, for the common good. I believe my life, and yours, is filtered through sovereign fingers given at His good measure.

79

So, do we make the choice or does the Father's leading take us where we belong?

I think you know my answer...

Now to each one the manifestation of the Spirit is given for the common good.
1 Corinthians 12:7 NIV

We lost our home due to major medical expenses
resulting from our youngest son's illness.
The Bible study that met in our farmhouse
came forward to help us build another.
Following the passage from the book of Nehemiah
to arise and build, we joined together
for a Pennsylvania house raising,
similar to the tradition of the nearby Amish barn raising.
God built our home and an everlasting bond
through the body of Christ.

The House that Built Us

The old farmhouse that was once our home has been renovated beyond recognition, but for me it remains untouched by time. When I ride past the old homestead, I see the long-ago picture of my children climbing trees and playing in snow-drifted cornfields. I look past the stone walls to my memories stored inside.

Trees have been leveled and replaced with asphalt, but my eye sees towering mulberry trees that once lined the dirt path leading up to the old red barn. The cornfield is littered with homes and activity, but my ear hears the soft chant of cicadas among tall stalks when babies snuggled with mama in the porch rocker.

When I was growing up in Bucks County, I longed to one day live in an old farmhouse. There was always the smell of brewed coffee and fried bacon at the farmhouse over the hills where mom sent me to buy eggs and butter. I wanted to live there.

Shortly after my husband, Jeff, and I married in the late seventies, we relocated to a rural community and found the classic Pennsylvania farmhouse to rent. It definitely needed a do-over. It was a beautiful mess. The charm of creaky wood floors and noisy screen doors our children burst through for playtime made it my dream home.

When I first glanced through the cracked windowpane of the neglected house, I could see it was in dire need of soap and love. It didn't take long for me, with my mother and daughter's help, to create a warm haven for our family. The house, filled with the scent of welcome-home from woodstove and cider, quickly became a refuge. The door remained unlocked, ready to receive anyone who needed a place to stay.

A tire swing hung from an old gnarled elm embracing all four of our laughing children at the same time. It's sad to see the tree is gone now, because the rings on the massive trunk not only revealed the age of the tree, but also the house with portions dating back to 1643. I mentioned I wanted an *old* farmhouse.

Shortly after moving in, a group of young people from our church asked if we would consider having our house be the meeting place for a weekly Bible study. We were thrilled because we had little kids and it would be convenient for everyone to meet at our place.

It was definitely a house made for large gatherings. A huge dining room, living room, and large study were next to the summer kitchen. Downstairs held a lot of people comfortably, and over time the group grew to more than forty people every Tuesday night. Our kids recall falling asleep to the many voices singing praise songs. We must have sounded like a choir.

A collection of good years in simple times, but not without countless challenges.

This is the home where our fourth child was born. Sadly, our baby was born with kidney failure, and the bills began to quickly mount up past our income. In addition to the six of us, we made a home for quite a few animals. Dogs, barn cats, bunnies, chickens, and goats added to our crowd. We couldn't imagine having to leave this sweet homestead.

We made countless repairs to mend the broken house, hoping to someday purchase it although we knew due to our finances it would be nearly impossible to purchase the house and fourteen acres. So, we were content to rent. But rentals can be temporary.

I dreaded having to move one day.

One morning while hanging the wash, a somber man dressed in black pulled up in a black car. Looked pretty bleak. He walked over to the clothesline without much introduction and dryly stated, "The local historical society is interested in purchasing this property to develop into a museum."

A museum? Seriously?

He continued with further explanation of the plans, but my overwhelming thoughts muffled the rest of his conversation. He went on anyway. "Someone will be in contact with you to let you know the date you'll need to vacate."

It was the kind of moment you remember just where you were when you heard what you didn't want to hear. Key word being "vacate."

Drowning him out while silently babbling to myself, I wondered where we'd go and how soon we would need to leave. How could we afford another home with the hospital expenses? No answers came with my solo dialogue.

I looked over at the old gnarly elm with the empty tire swing and asked out loud, "Are you hearing this, Lord?"

Weeks later, it was official. We had a deadline and had to move. Jeff and I privately agonized asking for direction, until we shared our concern with the Bible study gang at our next meeting. Praying with them helped remove some of the insecurities of losing our home. We knew God must have a better plan. We had to trust because we had experienced His provision countless times before.

I opened the Bible to a verse from the book of Nehemiah. Believing it was an answer, I read, "The God of heaven will give us success. Therefore, we will arise and build" (2:20). Jim, our study leader, lifted his bowed head and quietly asked, "Why not have a house raising like the Amish have barn raisings?"

Jeff and I looked at one another. Jeff answered with a "you're kidding" look on his face. "Yes, but they know what they're doing. I've never built anything but a car engine!"

Grateful for the generous offer, but convinced it would be a huge undertaking with or without help, we decided to pray and wait for further direction.

Not surprisingly, within a few short weeks we heard of a local seminar coming to our area for independent homebuilders. So, we had to go, right? After attending, we were reminded of another passage from Nehemiah. "I told them how the hand of my God had been favorable to me. Then they said, 'Let us arise and build, so they put their hands to the good work'" (Nehemiah 2:6). Okay, now I got it.

We couldn't wait to meet with our friends again to share our decision. They were delighted and more than willing. So, we stepped out in faith...

We began with a weary search for land near our church and schools. Nothing seemed right. Too far, too expensive, ground wouldn't perc, no owner financing. At last we found a large piece of land at the end of a dirt road. The location wasn't great except for the cornfields that hugged it on all sides. Finally, we were convinced that this was the assigned piece of earth for our project.

We bid low on the property. We had to. Of course, the offer was rejected. The landowner made a hasty exit out of the real estate office, and we figured that was that. But silently I prayed his heart would be changed. We knew only One who changes hearts. Before long, he came back without a smile and reluctantly accepted our meager offer.

God winked with a holy thumbs up.

It's hard work clearing a virgin site that has never been plowed. Teenage daughter and son wrestled brush hogs to clear the heavy thickness of briars and thorns. After weeks of toil, the ground was groomed and ready for our Bible study gang to carpool up to the promised land. Standing under watchful stars in the October chill, we held hands and asked a blessing to begin the work.

So, where to begin when a pile of lumber is dumped next to a huge hole in the ground?

Maybe like Noah, with nothing but a holy blueprint and cubits.

The next months were not easy for Jeff, holding down his day job and coming home to do another in the dark, in the cold heart of winter. Somehow, God placed a will and skill within him to carry out His purpose in the evenings with only a glimmer from a lantern and moonlight.

The sound of a solitary hammer turned into a symphony of pounding when our friends joined in. The endless faithfulness of calloused helping hands coated with sawdust, nights and weekends, made up the small God-designed crew from our Bible study group. A carpenter, electrician, plumber, and a mason.

The unity of working together was building us along with the house. We resisted the opposition of freezing temperatures, sickness, finances, and the delay of material delivery.

We had a deadline, but we had God's timing.

Our friend, the mason, slept near the cold edge of the poured foundation on January nights to guard the concrete while it cured. It's more than a faithful friend who sacrifices comfort to sleep in a house without walls.

Our friend, the carpenter, donated free labor and spent weeks framing our home. It's more than a faithful friend who lays aside his personal work to put another's need before his own.

While men labored, women cooked meals and cared for the children. A church friend who lived up the road left for work an hour early each day to work on our house. Everyone helped. Our teenage son and daughter spackled walls. Our baby sons splashed basement walls with waterproof coating. God used His people of all ages to erect the house to move in condition.

We met the deadline ahead of schedule!

Then, more opposition crept in when we applied for final financing. Unbelievably, we were denied a mortgage due to the high medical expenses. Months of sweat equity saturated each board, only to be told the home built with the work of our hands would not be ours. Our hearts fell to the earth it stood on.

I called the bank and immediately requested a meeting with the president. Unheard of!

The following day I received a call from the bank president who kindly told me he was aware of our personal situation and agreed to meet with me. I lined his desk with paper proof to show we were meeting our bills (hardly) despite the ongoing debt. He had to know after months of toil we would find a way! He took it before a committee who denied the request.

Denied-the-request.

Meanwhile, he received a phone call from someone in our church who asked to remain anonymous. They offered to pay a portion of the mortgage every month! It's more than a faithful friend who makes such an extravagant offer. It is a heavenly source poured out onto desperation.

The story of Nehemiah tells how God invited him to save the city. Our story tells how God used His body, gathering in an old farmhouse once a week, to save a family. Our church family has faithfully prayed and supported us through decades of crisis.

Radical grace displayed through a small group of loving friends who the Father brought together *for such a time as then.*

And since...

Two women from this circle later donated a kidney for our son years after mine failed him. Yes, it is more than faithful friends who sacrifice themselves—it is the amazing body of Christ.

We remain forever grateful for the ordinary, extra-ordinary people who God brought together to meet in an old farmhouse back in 1980.

The *museum* that stores a precious collection—our memories.

Crumbs

These are the crumbs we gather and store forever, the ones that lead to the greatness of God. I understood the desperate straits of those who lost jobs and homes due to circumstances beyond their control. What could we do?

It took a huge step of faith to go forward with God and only our friends to build a house. My trust started to waver when it appeared so far from our ability. It took a bigger step of faith when we finished and were denied a mortgage to move in. Although we were limited, God's provision was not.

What has God called you to do
that is beyond your ability?

**Unless the LORD builds the house,
they labor in vain who build it.**
Psalm 127:1

Womb waves, creating a life connection.
He is as far away as the end of the umbilical cord for now.
His little heart beats because mine does.
My heart breaks because his does.
What happens to the one on the other end of the cord,
when baby boy leaves as a prodigal?

The Son Who Left Home

"Mom, I found Tommy's wallet lying in the yard!" our eight-year-old, Shane, shouted. A wallet containing his driver's license and ten dollars was all our seventeen-year-old son meant to carry with him on his escape into the world.

The fallen wallet lying in the snow beneath the open window of Tom's empty room was the first clue of his hasty departure. A message scrawled on a scrap of paper placed on his unmade bed confirmed my fears. Our oldest son wrote, "I don't belong here any longer."

I read the note, wiping the tears pouring over my heart. What reason did he have to leave us? Did he need one? I stood lifeless in the center of his room, remembering clearly the small voice of the little boy who said, "Mommy, I'll love you infinity."

Infinity had come to a harsh end.

I knew the pain of rejection, but nothing compares to the rejection by one who once resided within.

89

We raise our children to leave us. From the moment they vacate the womb, we try to teach them how to meet the challenges of the world. Our heart accompanies them on the *days of firsts*. If you're a mom, you know the feeling of the first day of preschool, the first date, the college farewell, the wedding day—all cherished stepping-stones launching them into an independent life. But that same heart breaks wide open when a wayward child leaves home a prodigal with no intention other than to wander. Maybe that's why the word *prodigal* means waste.

The gospel of Luke tells the story of the son who left home to waste money, his good name, and his abilities. It became our son's story.

Tom left home in the night to begin a long and arduous journey. The good son who came to the crossroad chose the path that would take him far from his secure home and private Christian education. He forfeited an art scholarship to a nearby college in order to live with the family of a young girl he'd met the summer after high school graduation. It took weeks for us to locate Tom. Finally, my husband and I went to the home where he was staying and tried to reason with him.

Not knowing how we would be received, I prayed harder than the loud banging on the door. An unknown foot-in-the-door made it obvious we weren't welcome. Finally our son appeared to make us feel like intruders. We asked if we could talk with him, but he was unwilling.

Before we were shuffled out of the threshold, his dad said, "I hate the things you're doing, but I can never hate my son. You are loved and always welcome to come home, and I hope you'll do that now."

Tom became defensive and asked us to leave.

Broken and confused, we drove home to tell our

children that their brother was not coming home. We didn't hear from him for over nine months. Nine months. *Would I ever stop crying when I passed by the pictures of his life hanging on the wall?*

After Tom joined the Air Force, we received a few short letters. Each one was like a key to unlock the closed places between us. The postmarks told of his travels across the country. He seemed to make a point of calling on the nights when he'd been drinking. As much as I longed to hear from him, this only deepened the wound.

After restless hours, I'd leave my bed to shut myself outside in the night where my family couldn't hear me crying. Sitting on the kids' swing set, I would stare straight up into the night sky knowing the same stars covering me were covering him. The same Father covering me was covering him. I could almost hear the haunting melody from the Linda Ronstadt song, "Somewhere Out There."

My son had to feel my prayers.

About the same time Tommy left home a prodigal, our daughter left home a missionary. The close relationship they'd shared as children was severed as they went two separate ways. The dynamics of our family changed overnight. Tom continued on a mission to nowhere, while our daughter was on a mission in another country.

What did we do wrong? What did we do right?

We blamed ourselves. We blamed him. Maybe, we blamed God.

Failed relationships and broken marriages cut raw-deep into Tom's broken heart, filling years with more pain. Prayers and tears flowed unceasingly for this beloved son. I prayed with other parents of prodigals who understood my pain and faithfully joined me in deep intercession for him. I knew I had to pray the impossible—to let go and let God.

So, we waited for our son's return.

What would it look like? I wondered. I imagined how it would be. Watching for his familiar silhouette to come up the long expanse of our driveway. Would I run to him as the Father raced to meet me in my prodigal years? Would I embrace him against the womb where I held him safely for nine months? Or, would I stand there with arms folded, tapping my foot, defrosting slowly, asking why it had taken so long for him to come to his senses?

I prayed for a heart to meet him just where he was...

Later, our younger sons wandered for a time. The wonder years where all I could do was wonder if the love and dedication had been in vain.

The book of Proverbs teaches, "If we train up our child in the way he should go, when he is old he will not depart from it" (22:6). But as hurting parents, how do we survive in the interim?

Tough lessons came during times of testing. Struggles with abandonment, alcohol, drugs, prison, and divorce brought shame and division. I fasted and travailed. Yet, in the midst of the worst times, I continued to view my children as an inheritance and gift from God.

When Tom finally returned home, his Dad and I opened our arms and ran to him. We came to an understanding, and he stayed for a short time. But he soon left.

I know the pain we experience when a prodigal leaves home, but when a wanderer remains in the home the distress is far worse. Do we ask them to leave when they relentlessly alter our lives? When it pours out onto younger siblings? And what happens when they return only with regrets but not necessarily repentance? It is a time to choose battles wisely.

Too often, we place God the Father in the small image of our flawed earthly father, but Jesus says God is like *the* Father in Luke 15. The son ruptures the relationship and brings disgrace, but God the Father swiftly takes us in His arms to offer healing and restoration.

He doesn't wait with folded arms, tapping a holy foot. He runs to meet us!

He gathers up His robe and sprints to welcome the long-awaited son. He gives the lost child a kiss of greeting even though the foul scent of the pigpen lingers on him. Patiently and expectantly, He waits for our return at the foot of the cross as we eagerly waited for Tommy to appear at the foot of the driveway.

He did again...and again. As we, too, return to God after each of our sins. The account of the prodigal doesn't end when he returns. It continues with the Father's grace and delight in the child who has buried his head in the Forgiver's chest.

Crumbs

We expect our children to leave our home one day, but not to leave our life.

I questioned why God allowed one more hurtful thing to happen. In time I saw broader than my narrow view. The bigger picture was of the unconditional love we receive from a loving Father who teaches us how to love our children in the same way.

Have you experienced pain so great
you didn't know if you would heal?

"Can a woman forget her nursing child
And have no compassion on the son of her womb?
Even these may forget, but I will not forget you.
Behold, I have inscribed you
on the palms of My hands."

Isaiah 49:15

Elbows On My Bed

I was but a youth and thoughtless
as youth are apt to be,
Though I had a Christian mother
who had taught me carefully.

But there came a time when pleasures
of the world came to allure,
And I no more sought the guidance
of her love so good and pure.

Her tender admonitions
fell but lightly on my ear.
And for the gentle warnings
I felt an inward sneer.

But mother would not yield her boy
to Satan's sinful sway,
And though I spurned her counsel
she knew a better way.

No more she tried to caution
of ways she knew were vain,
And though I guessed her heartache
I could not know its pain.

She made my room her altar,
a place of secret prayer,
And there she took her burden
and left it in His care.

And morning, noon, and evening
by that humble bedside low,
She sought the aid of Him,
who understands a mother's woe.
And I went my way unheeding,

careless of the life I led,
Until one day I noticed
prints of elbows on my bed.

Then I knew that she had been there,
praying for her wayward boy,
Who for the love of worldly pleasure
would her peace of mind destroy.

While I wrestled with my conscience,
Mother wrestled still in prayer,
Till that little room seemed hallowed
because so oft she met Him there.

With her God she held her fortress,
and though not a word she said,
My stubborn heart was broken
by those imprints on my bed.

Long the conflict raged within me,
sin against my mother's prayer.
Sin must yield, for mother never,
while she daily met Him there.

Mother-love and God-love
are a combination rare,
And ones that can't be beaten
when sealed in earnest prayer.

And so at last the fight was won,
and I to Christ was led,
And Mother's prayers were answered
by her elbows on my bed.

Author Unknown

When faith was a seed and life overturned,
the cornfield was the sacred place of solitude
where I desperately sought the sound of God.

Voice in the Cornfield

There have been times I've felt like running farther than away. I thought everything would be okay if I could just find a new place, a new family, and a new me.

You may have been there. You may be there now. We can get as far as the edge of the planet, but we're still there. We will always be with ourselves.

Where can we run when the predators of life come too near?

I don't know of anyone who has the power to change my situation, but I do know of those I can go to who have experienced painful times. During a short break between crises, I spent the day with close friend, Karen. She seemed to always have the right word.

Over lunch, chatting about the trivial, she looked up from her teacup and quietly asked, "What do you do when the roof isn't caving in? Ya know, when you're not going through the major stuff?"

Hmmm...I had to think for a moment.

"I guess I just dwell in the cornfield where the roof doesn't cave in," I answered just to have something to say.

She gave a look of understanding and then used an example from the Bible of someone who experienced a few crises of his own.

If you are familiar with Daniel's story (he has his own book), you may remember he had a few big moments. The unforgettable lion's den, the vegan diet when he dared to say no to the king's rich menu, and interpreting Nebuchadnezzar's dreams. Good question. What was he doing in between the den-diet-and-dreams drama?

Praying deep. That's what he was doing...

He went home to his upstairs room where the windows opened toward Jerusalem. Three times a day he got down on his knees and prayed, giving thanks to God just as he had done before (Daniel 6:10).

Do you see it? *Giving thanks to God just as he had done before...*

No matter what he was facing.

The story of Daniel is about a man, as finite and human as we are, but whose faith shut the mouth of lions (Hebrews 11:33).

We want the kind of faith that shuts the mouth of the devourer, but sometimes we have to face lions in order to get it. Like Daniel, our circumstances take us to places we never thought we'd have to go. Places where we learn to pray deep.

When life became too hard, I found solitude in the depth of a cornfield. Sounds crazy, I know, but everyone should have a special prayer closet. Mine is lined with stalks covering me from the sound of the world. Even in the dead of winter when the fields are as leveled as I am...I hear God's voice. It became the family warm-hearted joke to look for mom praying in the cornfield if I couldn't be found.

When it came time for my twelve-year-old son to receive his first kidney transplant and despair surrounded our family, I'd stand on the edge of the field to watch him run strong to his tree house. Yet doctors gave him a timeline to live. This is when I needed to go deeper into the cornfield...deeper into prayer. I admit, many times I spent chatting with the sky and thought only the ears of corn were listening.

I couldn't pray hard enough. I couldn't bow low enough. And I couldn't escape the trial.

It was *then* I learned to hear above the roar in my den. *Then...*

Not a secluded holy garden—just a field of corn. My place of solace.

Crumbs

A tangible crumb—a portrait of Daniel in the den hangs in our pastor's study. Light filters down on the eyes of the lions, fixed on Daniel, ready to devour. The same light shines down on the eyes of Daniel, fixed on God, ready to deliver.

I keep the picture painted in my mind when the roar gets too loud. We'll see beyond our circumstances if we fix our eyes on the God who controls the lions rather than the lions.

Do you need to look past the den of circumstances?

Let us run with endurance
the race that is set before us,
fixing our eyes on Jesus,
the author and perfecter of faith.

Hebrews 12:1-2

*An ordinary evening changed life forever
when my husband suffered a sudden cardiac arrest.
Pronounced brain dead, with no pulse or respiration,
we were urged to discontinue life support.
Believing in what God can do in seven days,
I chose to wait.*

If I Should Wake Before I Die

"I'm dying..."

The piercing sound of Jeff's weak voice suddenly interrupted my busyness. Was he joking?

Only moments before, I answered impatiently when he asked me to leave my paper work and come into the other room to watch the presidential election. I was trying to finish up after a long day at work. Feeling guilty, I joined him in front of the fire on what I thought was just an ordinary November evening. I expected the day to end in the way it began. Together. But it didn't.

Did I hear what I thought I heard him say?

I looked over to see life leave him. I was shocked. Slouched, head back, blank stare, he gasped a last breath. Rushing to his side, I called his name, took his pulse, called His name...

Frozen in place, it took everything to move my feet to get to the phone and call 911. I couldn't find the phone. It was upstairs in the sewing room. I would have to use the wall phone, the one with a cord. But then I couldn't stay by Jeff's side.

"I think my husband is dying and I don't know CPR. You'll have to instruct me!" I shouted at the emergency dispatcher as if she had never received an urgent call.

Calmly, she coached me through the routine, asking me to repeat the steps back to her in order to save my husband's life. *Okay, I can do this.* I was certain his heart had to be beating again, until I realized the sound was the loud pounding of my own. Surprisingly, my clumsy obedience worked. I got a pulse. Then a beat. Finally...a breath.

Anxiously, I waited for the sound of sirens to come and rescue Jeff...and me. It seemed longer than the eighteen minutes it actually took for the emergency team to arrive. After they began to care for him, I was free to call our four children who lived nearby. They emerged quickly onto a scene of colored flashes of light and urgent shouts.

We stood huddled in the kitchen away from the mayhem, praying silently. Experienced medics lost him despite assistance of equipment. No breath, and next to no heartbeat. Then someone shouted they got him back.

Why did I think I would never see anything in this room except for this unforgettable scene?

We followed the speeding ambulance to the hospital like a bodyguard convoy. Upon arrival, we were told Jeff's shallow breath ceased during transport. I sat in the waiting room with our children and pastor, wondering what was happening behind the door.

Hating the waiting room. Hating the door.

Finally, the doctor appeared. After the medical team made every attempt to resuscitate him, a faint pulse gave no hope for Jeff to live through the night. We were told he suffered cardiac arrest and fell into a coma. Hours passed before I was permitted to go back to the intensive care cubicle that housed his failing body. I read Scripture through the night into his deaf ear, above the eerie sounds of the mechanical breath of a respirator.

Breath was gone. Moans and machines resonated haunting sounds from the near dead on this floor. I wanted to leave. I wanted to stay.

Early the next morning, Jeff was declared brain dead. Monitors showed only minimal brain stem activity. Was this dead enough? The doctor explained to our family how rare it is to survive an event such as this, and even if that should happen, the best we could hope for would be nursing home care for a very different person in a vegetative state.

So, how do I pray? Do I pray for him to live? How do we let go and hold on at the same time?

"No matter what unfolds," I told myself, "God is good and His love continues."

In stillness, he remained rooted in place like a fallen oak. Holding Jeff's cold hand, I traveled back in my mind and took him with me. We visited places we had been and the ones we would never see. We revisited places we had been through together, and I imagined places I would have to go in life without him.

Gazing at this once-capable body now lying helpless, I realized he was a reflection of my life. I remembered how he rescued me from the painful place of divorce when I was left with three small children he quickly called his own. How we hugged and cried when my third child nearly died, and how we held tight during the painful miscarriage that followed shortly after. We'd been there to help the other one up when thrown down by heartbreak, including the birth of our son who was born with kidney failure.

Now frail and powerless, like a corpse without a crypt, ready to leave his life the way his son entered into it, connected with machines and wires. The once-strong frame of a man who built our house now appeared fetal, head tucked into chest, arms and legs recoiled as though waiting to exit a womb...or enter a tomb.

I tried to look past his ashen eyelids to where he was hiding. What happens to the one in the deep place of a coma? I only know what happens to the one who remains awake.

I didn't want to say good-bye to the one who shared my valley journey, who shared tears of sorrow and tears of joy.

The days passed slowly, as we waited for Jeff to live and not die. The intensive care staff permitted countless friends, co-workers, and our church family to sit with him, sing over him, and say the things they never got to say to him. Our oldest son wouldn't leave and slept faithfully outside his door. Our daughter stayed by his side, continually inserting praise music into the portable tape player, hoping to coax some kind of reaction.

"I'm afraid he's not listening, dear," said one of the nurses.

"I'll keep playing the music until I know that for sure," replied daughter.

Embraced by love from a circle of friends, something stirred when his loyal brothers of Girard arrived. Jeff was raised in Girard College, a Philadelphia orphanage enclosed by high stone walls, until he was eighteen years old. Throughout their lives all they had was one another. I stood in the corridor and watched these boys, now old men, surround one of their own with the same wall of protection they knew as children. Men bred of iron while in the stone cocoon. They whispered childhood memories into his ear, hoping to awaken his fading mind.

Would they be the key to unlock his sleep?

I felt lonely in the crowd.

Sitting quietly one morning in the hospital chapel, I turned to a passage from the book of Isaiah. "You were tired out by the length of your road, yet you did not say, 'It is hopeless.' You found renewed strength, therefore you did not faint" (Isaiah 57:10). But I wanted to faint. I wanted to escape.

As days progressed, it became impossible to hope. The social worker suggested the time had come to discontinue the ventilator. With her hand gently on mine, she said, "I'm sorry. There is no longer any need for life support. We need to be kind and let him go."

Taking a deep breath of my own, I firmly replied, "I know what God can do in seven days. We'll wait."

I noticed a tear on Jeff's pale cheek. He must've heard. Couldn't the nurses see? How could he possibly be brain dead when he understood enough to be heartbroken? Our sons and daughter surrounded their father, responding in their own way. Finally, son Tom said, "It's okay to go home now, Dad. I'll take care of Mom."

Another tear slid down the side of his face. A sign of life. A sign of a heart that still feels. We were sure he heard...

But well-meaning people confirmed there was no hope for him to survive. I actually received a few sympathy cards when it was posted on the time clock at work that he was already gone.

I believe with the holy breath and a spoken Word from

God our world was created. But with a breath and a spoken word from Jeff, my world returned.

A miracle.

On the morning of the seventh day, a new shift nurse entered his room asking questions as though she awaited a response from him. I appreciated her.

"Did you see the game yesterday, Mr. Bowman? Who's your favorite team?"

Silence.

She adjusted his feeding tube. Still chatting over his lifeless body, she maneuvered to change the soiled sheets.

More silence.

"Pittsburgh Steel-ers...," he slowly murmured.

Awe!

Did I hear what I thought I heard him say?

She hurried from the room calling out to the nurses' station for someone to page the cardiologist. The medical team rushed in. Examining Jeff, the doctor quietly asked, "Do you know what happened to you?"

Jeff mumbled a slurred, "No..."

The doctor didn't go into detail, but described how he suddenly lost consciousness the week before while in his home watching television. Jeff looked up somewhat confused and said, "It must've been the frying pan!" suggesting I knocked him out.

Between wonder and laughter, the doctors and nurses assured us they rarely witness full restoration after a near-fatal event, but never knew anyone to wake up with a joke!

November slowly turned into December. Soon after he was stabilized, Jeff was transferred to an acute rehab center in Philadelphia for weeks. Then came Christmas shopping in a wheelchair. Next, walking by the turn of a new year. With time and therapy the crisis passed us by. But the grace remains forever in how God speaks life into lifeless situations.

Although Jeff can't recall the words spoken to him during his seven-day sleep, he clearly heard a message of love from all those who surrounded him and his family that helped to bring him back to life. The memory is stored in his heart, which now beats quite steadily with the help of an implanted defibrillator tucked inside his chest.

Crumbs

You can imagine, this was a most special holiday for our family. I believe Christmas is a time when strange and wonderful things happen. Long ago, wise and royal visitors came riding in the lunar light of a shining star and God came down to earth as a Holy Child to live among us. Immanuel. God is with us, not just in the holy season but in the everyday that doesn't always turn out like we planned.

Can you believe when it's hard to believe?

**And Jesus answered saying to them,
"Have faith in God."**
Mark 11:22

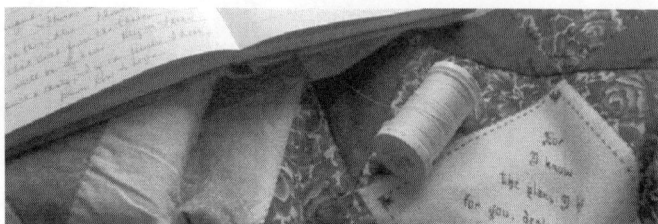

This too shall pass,
but while it's here
I want to learn from it.

The call that every parent dreads
came in the middle of a rainy night when our son
was in a near fatal car accident.
Unidentifiable and medivaced to a trauma center,
he was admitted as John Doe
and not expected to survive the night.

A Call in the Night

"Mrs. Bowman, we believe we have your son in our trauma center and need you to come as soon as possible to identify him." The words were like an electric current forcing me to drop the phone and run.

Just a short time earlier I woke to a silent scream. The alarm that only a mom hears. I rolled over and stared at 1:13 a.m. illuminated on the bedside clock. With heart pounding, I listened to the rain beating against the windowpane. The dull glow from the desk lamp in the foyer confirmed my fear that Shane had not come home.

Sleep was impossible. It wasn't a night where I could stay in the comfort of my bed and pray. I had to get up. I had to kneel and cry out for his safe return. It was not his pattern to stay out late on a work night, but he had been making a series of poor choices lately. Creating a mental hit list of what I'd say when he walked in, I had to guard my mind from empty imagination.

Kneeling by the chair, I opened my Bible and saw the

caption above Psalm 16: "The Lord is our portion in life and deliverer in death." When I read these words, nothing else mattered except that he came home. For nearly two hours, I prayed and believed for his safe return.

At 3:10 a.m. the shrill ring of the phone echoed throughout the house. I walked to the kitchen in slow motion, not wanting to pick up the receiver, trying to prepare for what I would hear. Somehow I knew it would not be my son's voice saying he had a flat tire. Instead, a hospital chaplain calmly stated that a young man presumed to be our son had been medivaced to their facility. Unable to be identified, he had been admitted as John Doe.

He was not expected to live.

My husband and I drove to the hospital in silence. What can you say when your son is delivered to the emergency room nameless and dismembered?

Finally, I spoke out in the stillness of the car. "When did it happen, Father? Was it at 1:13 when I was abruptly awakened from sleep to pray? Was that when my child's blood spilled out on the highway?"

More silence.

Riding in the quiet with no sound except the repetitive murmur of wiper blades, I reviewed the past months since Shane moved back home. Troubled by his painful divorce and separation from his daughter, he had become more distant. Totally unarmed, I went into speculation mode... Could this have been a result of drinking? Did he finally break?

We pulled into the hospital parking lot. I fell in step with my husband, numbly walking inside and down the hollow corridor to see what remained of my son. We were told Shane had stopped breathing while waiting for the helicopter to arrive. To our disbelief, his ex-brother-in-law was one of the emergency crew who came to the accident site. He didn't recognize Shane.

I stood in the threshold for a minute, hoping my feet would take me to his side. Leaning close, I spoke into his ear and stroked his blood matted hair, reassuring him I was there even though I wasn't sure he was...

Ignoring the early hour, I called our assistant pastor. Immediately he came with his wife and remained in the waiting room while we stood by Shane's bed. I called two close friends, Glenda and Karen. These are the kind of friends who are on the night watch with you. Glenda shared a Scripture from Ezekiel 16:6. "When I passed by you and saw you squirming in your blood, I said to you while you were in your blood, 'Live!'"

Jeff and I continued to pray this verse over our son during the lengthy bedside vigil. Sitting next to this young man broken in body and spirit, still appearing comatose, he gently squeezed my hand at the sound of my voice. My prayer continued. "Let him respond to Your voice, Father, in a way he never has before."

All of his personal belongings had been discarded after his arrival. Why not? None of the attending physicians expected him to survive. His bloodstained leather jacket was the only thing returned to us. I wanted what was left of my son and retrieved the remnants of torn clothing from the receptacle.

The following day his dad examined the accident scene. Jeff sat in shock as he imagined what Shane's last thoughts must have been. He recovered his watch in a nearby field close to the highway. Only the crystal was broken. It had stopped at 11:22 that October night, seconds before the steering column punctured his chest.

The speedometer inside the mangled metal stopped at 42 mph. Not too fast, not too late. Yet, too late for anyone to save him.

What could have caused this tragedy? Another driver?

Days later we learned alcohol was involved. Shane stopped at a sports bar on the way home from work. Downpours of rain and thick fog made this a fatal mix as he crossed over the hidden lane into the path of an oncoming car.

I was angry. I was crushed.

The blur of passing days spun into a week, a month, and left the calendar pages unturned on the side of the refrigerator. Home was a place I visited from time to time, but it only reminded me of his absence—*of the call in the night.*

During the next three months, Shane remained in the Intensive Care Unit at the trauma center. I kept a faithful log of God's continued work of mercy as I sat hour after endless hour. The reams of paper entries sustained me as we encountered the altered hours from jobs, family, and each other.

Finally, the doctors confessed, "We have done all that is in our power. There's nothing left that we haven't done."

Shane's pelvis was blown apart. His right foot was crushed to powdered bone with no hope of preserving it. He was kept in a drug-induced coma, weeks of stillness, as they tried to repair his torso. He was girded in a body cast except for one arm, the only one they could use to draw blood for months. Multiple organs were lacerated and ruptured. He needed to stay sedated. My cry was, "Sedate me, Lord!"

The social worker informed us we would not be able to care for him at home and advised that he be moved to a nursing home due to the minimal possibility he would ever walk again. We refused. I filed an appeal, and he remained in ICU.

We could scarcely walk ourselves after listening to another morbid prognosis. He had been actively involved in sports since he was a young boy. We didn't know how we would tell him.

He underwent six surgeries in the next seven weeks, an unceasing attempt to repair the severed internal organs. Each failed. The doctors explained it was like stitching frayed fabric that refused to hold together.

As a last resort, it was decided they would transport him to Duke University in North Carolina. Once again, it was evident that we could rely only on God and His powerful intervention.

This was not the first time we had been confronted with man's limitation. By now the medical team was fresh out of ideas, and we were fresh out of knowing how to pray. It was at this desperate moment in our weakness that we depended on the prayers of our intercessors.

Often we pray to be delivered from calamities. We even trust that we will be; however, we find it is in these times we feel Him nearest.

> *I will lift up my eyes to the mountains;*
> *From where will my help come?*
> *My help comes from the LORD,*
> *Who made heaven and earth.*
> Psalm 121:1–2

After long months of rehabilitation, Shane showed some improvement and was able to walk with the assistance of a nurse on either side. His father looked on with tears of joy at this far greater step than his first one as a toddler! The unexplainable, walking on a foot crushed to dust. Yet, God created an entire man from dust! The mystery we try and explain...or dismiss.

Shane returned home a changed person, unlike when he left on the unforgettable night in the storm. I've often found this to be true in the storms permitted in our lives. We never exit the same way we enter. There is a lesson behind every trial.

The months of suffering in the hospital, while a triumph of faith and healing, turned out to be only the forerunner to the months of suffering yet to come.

It had been a year of trial and triumph. A bitter mix of joy and sorrow escorted us through the long months of recovery leading up to the impending threat of a jail sentence.

I surfed my journals reviewing past trials that God had brought us through, asking God for one more mercy.

☙✷❧

Just when I felt my lowest, I revisited another bleak time when we were told Shane was not expected to live.

At twenty months old, Shane contracted a rare condition called epiglottitis. This is a disease where the airway becomes sealed off, making it difficult to breathe. It can quickly turn deadly.

Time can never dim the near loss of a child. That unforgettable day, my little boy had been playing contentedly on the kitchen floor. My prayer time that morning left me with an uneasy feeling concerning him.

Although there were no symptoms of illness, I called the doctor's office. They saw no reason to have me bring him in. I knew better. I hung up the phone and drove to the pediatrician's office. Upon examination, the doctor turned pale with surprise and immediately had him rushed to the hospital where an emergency tracheotomy was performed.

Helplessly sitting in the waiting room, an urgent voice blared over the intercom, "Code Blue!" Immediately, I ran to the nurses' station to ask if the alert was concerning my child. Hesitantly she stammered, "Yes, I'm sorry...they're doing everything possible." Later, I was told the wrong size trach tube had been inserted in Shane's tiny lung, perforating the wall. The other lung was torn.

He was not expected to live.

The waiting room was suddenly converted into a private maze with nowhere to turn. Alone and new to the area, I'd called a local pastor whose church I'd visited the Sunday before. He hurried to the hospital and remained by Shane's crib, praying and anointing him with oil. Fairly new in my faith, I had no clue what he was doing.

Hours later, x-rays showed the lungs began to heal. Within three days he was sent home! He was featured in the church newsletter as "the miracle baby." This powerful demonstration of God's intervention in raising the desperately ill was only the beginning of what would occur in the life of our family.

ʕ.♥.ʕ

Shane's close brush with death as a child and as a man caused me to realize how miraculously God spared him twice. Remembrance of these amazing events allowed me to face the day of Shane's court appearance. Forearmed in prayer, I surrendered the outcome to God. "Your will be done," was my simple prayer.

Shane received a ten-month sentence, was bound in handcuffs, and led away. I drove home alone feeling just as bound. It was difficult to tell the others waiting at home. He may have been the one in the car, but our family was in the wreck.

Slowly, autumn turned into winter. The sound of iron bars locking our son away from us echoed in my head night and day. Our family gathered for Thanksgiving with one less. The empty chair was a tortured sign of his absence.

Shane's six-year-old daughter visited her dad in the hospital, but not while he was in the correctional center. He ached to see her. On Christmas Day, he was granted a pass to visit us. Finally, the day came when we could see him. For three hours.

For much of my Christian life I struggled with control. This was the toughest lesson in how to surrender all things to the One who does control all things. I had to genuinely lay my son on the altar and entrust him to God's merciful care. Only His timing reaches the exact minute it takes to carry out the unique plan He has for us. Shane found freedom in a cell and developed strength and character that brought him to the other side of his journey victoriously. It was a long road that seemed to have no end.

ᴧ.ᴠ.ᴄ

Looking back, I compare Shane's story to the view outside my office window. A wavering tree branch begins to dress for spring. Only weeks before, the branch lay heavy-laden with ice, bending low as if to break. Though frail, the branch endured the violent winter winds and became strong. Now its blossoms and fruit appear.

The call in the night came before the phone actually rang on the night that will never be erased. The voice of the Father called me awake to be the prayer covering over my son in his desperate time of need.

Part of me sways on the bitter edge and asks, "Why?" I call to mind the words of Psalm 16 that spoke to me on the October night when the phone rang. The emptiness may never leave. Perhaps that is the scar I bear as a mother. But I'm reminded of Another's scars and how His wounds continue to heal ours.

There are many scars on my son's body, but I don't see the marks of a surgeon's knife. Instead, I see the loving marks of where God laid His hands to pour life back into broken places.

May He continue to use our mistakes to shape us into the image of His Son.

Crumbs

I often pass by the stretch of road where my son had the accident. It is a huge marker on my path that taught me to depend only on an unlimited Father in heaven. Man could not help. I had to look further than what I was seeing—a broken son who had no hope. I had to envision him whole, even if it meant he wouldn't be healed.

At the time of this incident, I was recovering from a double surgery. My youngest son was rejecting a kidney and in need of another transplant. A few months earlier, my husband had suffered multiple strokes. The crumbs on this portion of my dark path were the lights leading me to a deeper place of dependence on God and the body of Christ.

When have you experienced something
that seemed beyond repair?

I will bless the LORD who has counseled me;
Indeed my mind instructs me in the night...
Because He is at my right hand, I will not be shaken.
Psalm 16:7–8

*Coping with multiple medical conditions in our family
grew more challenging when I became afflicted
with a personal thorn in the flesh.*

In the Middle of My Midnight

Picture a runner trying to reach the goal while on a tough course filled with obstacles. What keeps them from giving up? We make the choice to overcome the things that cripple our gait or choose to simply surrender. This was a time I struggled to stay in the race.

The impact a child's lifelong illness has on a family is difficult to explain to someone who hasn't experienced it.

From infancy until he was thirteen years old, I made the trip with Geoffrey to an inner-city hospital three times a week, two times a week, and as he got older, once a month. Following his first transplant, the cycle of multiple hospital visits started all over again. It was a bitter mix, but I was grateful for the bond connecting us closely during those times.

Although our family life was often centered around hospitals, a huge interruption in our lives occurred when my husband became ill with bladder cancer for the first time. A few years later he was diagnosed with heart disease and suffered multiple strokes and cardiac arrest, resulting in a coma. It was hard.

There were times I asked if life was more over than it had been. I actually feared God's plan for my life.

Medical problems continued to add to the difficulties we were already experiencing, but it didn't change our attempts to keep things normal and upbeat. Even in the dark times, family and laughter were a priority.

But then...one more...

I could hardly get out of bed one morning. My legs wouldn't take me down the stairs. Holding the banister, I took one step at a time, like a child. Since it came on so suddenly, I thought it might be Lyme disease. Months of visits to specialists and blood work confirmed a diagnosis of rheumatoid arthritis. Being the caregiver for others was suddenly altered by my personal affliction.

When I was young, I thought arthritis was something every old person complained about in rainy weather. I quickly learned RA, an autoimmune disease, is not only about crippled joints but it also affects the organs, especially the heart and lungs. The immune system becomes the enemy of the body it is supposed to protect.

I had a feeling of panic when I wasn't able to take care of my own needs. Before I knew the extent of what happened, I was unable to brush my teeth, zip my jeans, turn the key in the ignition, hold a coffee cup, or open a door after it was closed. I couldn't walk without feeling like I was on a road of broken glass. I didn't think it could get worse until one day I was unable to pick up my crying grandchild. I understood why those afflicted with this disease battle depression.

I did everything I knew to make myself better, starting with having the elders of my church anoint me with oil. I researched my illness to the same extent that I did my son's when he was born with renal disease. I took an aggressive route with nutrition, juicing, homeopathic doctors, specialists, and finally having to submit to prescribed high-powered biologic medications costing thousands of dollars a month. Nothing helped the no-cure, no-hope prognosis. Twice a week I self-injected medicine I didn't want to use. I prayed for remission. Nothing changed.

When I read of the apostle Paul having an infirmity, I often wondered if it could have been arthritis. It sure felt like a thorn in the joints. Scripture doesn't say, except that a messenger of Satan sent some kind of affliction. It tells us Paul's "thorn in the flesh" was for his benefit and when asking God to remove it, the answer he received was "My grace is sufficient for you, for power is perfected in weakness" (2 Corinthians 12:9).

I thought this must be my answer, also.

What can we do when our body betrays us?

In 2010, I had two joints replaced in my right hand and reconstruction on my wrist. While persevering through ten months of physical therapy to restore the use of my hand, I sensed the Lord calling me to write. *Now?* So, I resigned from Women's Ministry to devote myself to writing. After years of journaling and writing articles for magazines, I believed it was time to write the book I had in my heart for quite some time.

Why would God ask me to write when I wasn't able to hold a pen? Again, I was reminded that His power is sufficient in my weakness.

While recuperating, the women of my Precept Bible study class pitched in to purchase speech recognition software for my computer. This was the answer! I began dictating pieces of my journals into written documents. The timing of the project was perfect (of course), because re-reading them was more healing than the physical therapy.

I find there is nothing I can do with a disease that has no cure except to believe for one. Rheumatoid arthritis screams pain throughout my body daily, but I have learned to cope with my thorn and take it one grace step at a time. I've learned to give what I can and receive what is given to me, an opportunity to help one another.

Crumbs

Broken hearts and bodies are often too much to bear, until we look at what it builds within us.

I struggle with the things I cannot do, but I concentrate more on the things I am able to do in spite of a limiting disease. It's a choice.

Have you ever felt limited?

And He has said to me,
"My grace is sufficient for you,
for power is perfected in weakness."
Most gladly, therefore,
I will rather boast about my weaknesses,
so that the power of Christ may dwell in me.
2 Corinthians 12:9

*The great grandfather I never knew in childhood
made an impact on my eternity.*

My Begats

We all want to know where and who we come from. I often wondered about the faded black-and-white images pasted for keeps on the pages of old family scrapbooks. Who were they, really? And if our features were similar, what other resemblances were there?

After all, every heritage trait that seems to run in the family has to come from someone more closely related than Adam and Eve. If I heard "the apple doesn't fall far from the tree" once, I heard it a thousand times while growing up. Everyone said how much I was just like my dad and my grandmother...*but never me.*

Once my grandchildren were born, I looked at the antique people in my background differently. I realized this is what I am to them—a person they may be "likened to." Will my life bring good to theirs by my actions today? And what about my yesterdays?

We hand things down. Have you ever noticed when you go to the doctor's office, you're asked, "Is there any history of heart disease, cancer, or diabetes? Pre-disposition doesn't only involve illness.

Sometime after I became a Christian, I met a woman of deep faith who told me the importance of breaking generational sin. I didn't know what she was talking about, but I wanted to find out. As I matured in my faith, I learned how to stand in the gap for the spiritual inheritance of my children. Confessing personal strongholds, I asked God to remove the negative legacy handed down from *me*. I prayed again when a new generation was placed within my daughter and sons, and more begats came along.

The greatest view we can behold is looking into the face of a grandchild and finding our child stamped onto another's flesh. I see my children in the faces of their children, and I'm a young mom once again filled with recycled memories.

While tracing the root system of my family tree, I discovered I was probably a first-generation Christian. Honestly, I couldn't identify one believer in my family. Not my parents, grandparents, aunts, uncles, until I remembered...one.

My mother's grandfather, a man I never met. I only saw him face-to-stoic-face on the pages of a small tattered scrapbook. All I knew of John Henry Carter was his love for the seaside of Cape May where my mother visited regularly as a child after her mother passed away. The old photographs revealed a regal man dressed in a period waistcoat, trimmed with a vintage pocket watch, bifocals balanced gracefully at the end of his nose. He looked like President Roosevelt. But what beat beneath the waistcoat was a heart for God.

I got to know the man between the lines of his letters. Unfortunately, as a teenager, his effort of faithfully writing to me wasn't appreciated. I didn't care about the words as much as the unique penmanship scripted on crisp parchment with the primal flair and elegance of a signer of the Declaration of Independence. He didn't simply write a letter, he made it a keepsake.

Dear child of my granddaughter,

Be pure in thought and deed. Beware of radio music, dance, and painting your face with the world. Let your life speak of Who you belong to.

Greetings from your great grandfather,

JH Carter

Sorry to say, I was doing all three while reading his warnings. I thought there had to be a warmer pen pal, but my mom insisted I politely answer each letter because he didn't write to the other great-grandchildren. He must've sensed a rebel. Reluctantly, I would reply with a short note about my stamp collection or runaway dog, and he'd quickly respond with another fire and brimstone message.

It took decades before I understood this man's concern about the eternal destiny of the next generation. A bit legalistic and old school, but he loved the Lord and prayed faithfully for his begats. The few paper heirlooms I've kept serve as a reminder that he may have been the solitary person praying for me…and mine.

Many times we're tempted to skip over the boring begat-beget-begots in the Bible. However, genealogies are important because they reveal the majesty of God's plan in the mysterious way He connects DNA into kin. He is a generational God, passionate to preserve His righteousness through the ages, and that's accomplished through future generations.

I look back to the influence my grandmother had in teaching me to trust in my own strength and compare that to the influence of this unknown ancestor leading me to the place where I found the true source of strength. How'd that happen?

In the book of Timothy, it tells the importance of a grandparent passing down faith to future generations. "I am reminded of your sincere faith, which first lived in your grandmother Lois and in your mother Eunice and, I am persuaded, now lives in you also" (2 Tim. 1:5 NIV).

Just think, if Timothy's grandparent had not been faithful in passing her faith to her daughter, and then to her grandson, we might be missing two books in the Bible.

Crumbs

The letters from my great-grandfather were crumbs I overlooked, but the words I disregarded became important to me years later.

I don't believe we recognize how our lives can impact the lives of those to come.

Good or bad.

So, I pray by name for our Japheth, Joah, Taleh, Brianna, and Avery and their begats. To my great-great-greats, I can leave a blessing or a curse by the way I live.

And so can you...

**One generation shall praise Your works to another,
And shall declare Your mighty acts.**
Psalm 145:4 NKJV

I've written, re-written, crumpled and tossed,
attempting to write the story I didn't want to live
or re-live on paper—the story of when death collides
with life. It's not easy sharing a life
when you've lived hidden...and exposed.
Living in a glasshouse, in a glass church,
only grace washes clean what people see into,
so I learn to be transparent.

Till Death Do Us Part

2006. My mother was dying. My marriage was dying. My son's kidney was dying.

And I think my faith was dying.

Try to understand.

My life was devastated by a perfect storm when three systems came together and leveled everything in its path. It all happened within a calendar page. I didn't know what to grieve first or most. Yet, sifting through the rubble, I found huge pieces of God.

My mother

Till death do us part was meaningful to my parents. They didn't do everything right, but they did commitment well. They made a vow not to break up in brokenness. In a way, I admired them even when they fought. They made up. They went on.

My parents were a strong example of what devotion looks like, but I didn't see it in my personal life. The twisted script of my marriage vows has sometimes read *till I get over you, do us part.*

My mother wasn't a strong woman of faith until later in life, but she was always a faithful woman. I have a lasting picture in my mind of her graveside loyalty up to the time she passed away at age eighty-four. Losing her mother when she was fourteen years old, she never missed a special day in seventy years of seasons to place a remembrance on her grave.

My father passed away, leaving her a widow in her early fifties. She made the same steadfast pilgrimage to his gravesite every anniversary, birthday, the day they first met, and the day they last parted. By death.

In mid-March, a phone call came to our church office. The secretary came downstairs to the Bible study classroom to have me take a call from my mother's doctor.

I knew it had to be serious for him to track me down at church. I listened, unbelieving, as he pronounced a death sentence. "Myelogenous leukemia allows a person to live only six to eight weeks after diagnosis. I'm sorry."

It must be a mistake. She's fine.

Less than four weeks later, she was gone.

Wait. What?

Shortly after the diagnosis, she methodically finalized her life on earth. I received a call late one night asking me to take her to the hospital. By the time my oldest son and I fought heavy rain to arrive at her home, she had the bed made, dishes washed, and rent check written so she would owe no one after she was gone.

She said it wasn't necessary to pack a bag. Somehow, she knew she wasn't coming back home.

Before this night came, the most important thing was for her to visit my dad's grave one last time before it became her own. Easter was close to his birthday, and she seemed determined to place a lily on his grave. My daughter and I took her to the cemetery thirty-eight miles away to the generational burial place of our family. I hated to go there with my Grandmother Rose when I was a child. I hated it even more on this day. Now I was fetching water from the same antique spigot, in the same antique watering can, for my dying mother to water the flower she buried on her soon-to-be grave.

Walking down the familiar cemetery path, I can still see in the distance a strong woman with auburn hair, standing straight, wiping sorrow from her face, who soon became a gray-haired woman, bending low, and still wiping tears. Now, the white-haired woman, leaning hard on the stone marker with her beloved's name etched deep on granite where her glory-date would soon be recorded on the other side of the dash. Her white hair didn't reveal age. It revealed loyalty. Staring and dry-eyed, she was ready for the journey. Married to one man for life till his death...and hers.

She was a faithful mom to an only child, and I was a faithful child to my only mom. The last week of her life my daughter and I stayed by her side, lying in the hospital bed next to hers, listening to breath fade quickly, until...

Another phone call.

Something smelled foul within the sanitary stench of the hospital corridor when I picked up my husband's cell phone left in the waiting room. I listened to the familiar voice leave a message confirming betrayal. Betrayal comes in multi-colors; it's not always what we consider betrayal. But hurt is hurt. Deception is deception.

My marriage was dying with my mother.

Caught up in the whirlwind of emotion, I felt as though my insides would spill outside. Stand or faint— what to choose?

Heart weighed down, my legs barely took me back to my mother's room. Holding back tears, wearing the mask of composure I always keep nearby, I entered her room to see Sheri holding a hyacinth beneath her grandmother's ashen face. Mom smelled Easter one last time. Her eye fixed on the threshold, watching for me. Waiting... waiting for me to hold the one taking her final breath— the one who held me for my first.

My husband

Once again, life seemed over.

Wait. What?

What just happened in the hospital corridor? Somehow, my rescuer became my adversary.

It must be a mistake. We're fine.

Everything seemed fine until it wasn't. There was no warning for this storm, no forecast, no time to prepare. Jeff and I have gone through more than the average couple. Continually. How did we survive? We didn't.

What was too much for me, must've been too much for him...and we all fall down. Now, caught up in something bigger than him and bigger than us, there was no way out, but out. A man who once was strong enough to build a house for his family, foolishly laid down his armor to face his enemy with the strength of an old man. He lost the battle.

Trust shattered again. This time I was beginning to question if I could continue to trust God to bring good out of so much bad. I had to embrace the pain before it choked me dry. Once again, I was abandoned before we separated. This time, ready? No...but this time, Jesus.

My pastor, church elders, and sheltering friends walked me through death valley when I allowed them. Mostly, I ran to the silence...the sacred space where I could hear myself grow. I asked my pastor if I could take time away from teaching so acid didn't spill on others. I felt called to simply stand and wait during our seven-month separation.

I'm amazed in the way my children and grandchildren handled the series of tragedies in our family. But this time was different. I knew they were not only confused but also challenged to finally see the ones who stood strong through unbelievable circumstances finally crying uncle. Son Tom, always strong in a crisis, remained on both sides. My daughter was trying to deal with her personal loss of her grandmother while mopping up what was spilling out on her own family. My other sons stayed close in the middle of my night...mare. However, there are times when flesh and blood are just not real enough.

Only God could undo my undone.

Contented in my alone place, I thought I found peace. What's dead can stay dead, I thought. Until, startled awake one night with an unknown word...*retrovaille*. What does that mean? How do you spell it to even Google it? Somehow I did. Pronounced ret-ro-vi, a French term for rediscovery, I found it was a lifeline for those ready to divorce. Not a marriage encounter weekend, which we were far past, but a salvage ministry. I wrestled and resisted.

For months my husband faithfully went for counseling with a local pastor. I hoped it would matter more to me.

The well must be finally empty. I didn't want to hear how desperately he wanted to return.

*I wanted...*to grieve my mother's death without distraction. *I wanted...*to be on my face in prayer for my son who was rejecting a third kidney transplant. *I needed* to get right in my heart before I could do either.

The multiple trauma served as a catalyst taking me back to a dreaded place where I didn't want to return, facing things I thought had been conquered in my young life. The rotted remnant needed to go...altogether.

Reluctantly, I agreed to go to the Retrovaille weekend in Media followed by six intensive weeks learning how to survive a crisis. I hated every minute until the last two weeks. Finally, I understood the term re-discovery meant personally, not simply as a couple. Did I say *finally*?

The uncovering helped me learn about...me. It helped Jeff learn about Jeff.

Hurt and Healer continued to collide during the dismantling and rebuilding, yet the consuming battle for me remained my son...

My son

I spent so much of my time chasing solitude in Lancaster County during the separation from marriage, ministry, and life. Cornfields, my prayer closet, until...

I received another phone call. This time from a number I know well—the University of Pennsylvania Hospital. "Mrs. Bowman, we can't locate your son, and he's in trouble. His creatinine is 11.2. He's rejecting his kidney and needs to get here immediately for emergency dialysis."

Wait. What?

It must be a mistake. He's fine.

He had just returned from a cruise. He was the best man in his best friend's wedding. He met his wife-to-be. Only weeks before, he stood by his grandmother's coffin and everyone remarked how handsome and healthy he appeared. Can't be...now.

What could go so wrong, so fast?

Apparently, he was exposed to shingles while on the cruise, causing him to reject. I silently mentored myself in order to breathe, to think.

I think...I was out of prayers.

This was the first time in Geoff's life I faced this kind of news alone. Although it had been difficult for our entire family throughout years of hospitals and illness, Jeff was the only one who shared the same parent-pain. From the age of thirty-one, my life had been consumed praying and believing for my son's wellness. Defeated time after time, I had to sift through negative words spoken by physicians to hear the promises of a healing God.

And, Jeff was there...

How could everything be dying at once?

If God's big enough to control powerful forces of nature, He must be big enough to resolve this personal storm. My only choice was to believe again...and again.

I believe whatever our faith says God is, He will be. I still do.

But, honestly, I wondered if my life and faith had been in vain. My marriage of nearly thirty years had been interrupted. The son I prayed for continually for nearly the same amount of time, was in need of yet another kidney transplant. In the middle of it all, I lost my mom, the faithful one who had always been there. So, what was left?

God.

The months ahead were much like the months behind...broken into wholeness. I was grateful to come to the end of a relentless year of death, dialysis, and the ultimate rejection. The last page of my 2006 journal was blank with no miracle to record. Though I wished I could have written that my son received life into his failing body and Jeff and I received life into our failing marriage, I was unable at the time.

Instead, I had to be satisfied with the certainty of the true miracle of still standing in the middle of the loss. Realizing the gain.

Crumbs

By this time on my journey I had been following God for over thirty years, and yet I discovered more of His goodness, nearness, and power than anytime before in the midst of the strain. I felt desperate, distant, and devoured. There were many times along the way I was tempted to give up, but God in His faithfulness didn't let go.

Have you ever felt desperate?

*All the days of my struggle
I will wait until my change comes.*
Job 14:14

Looking back on my son's lifelong illness
while traveling to the hospital one night in expectation
of another kidney transplant, I prayed for him
not to receive.
How do we hold on to hope when we get to an open door that
suddenly closes and rusts shut with time?
Yet, I remain confident that God will not delay
one second beyond the appointed time.

Journey of a Lifetime in One Night

Traveling down the dark highway at 4:30 in the morning, I could scarcely see the familiar road through tears and the rain-glazed windshield.

My son, Geoff, phoned the night before to relay the long-awaited call from the hospital.

"Mom, there's a kidney available that matches perfectly! I need to be there early in the morning. Can you meet me at the hospital?"

We had been through this a few times, so before becoming too excited I asked the background of the deceased donor. Geoff sensed my hesitancy and admitted there was a questionable social and physical history. I didn't feel a peace about it, but he decided to go forward and contacted the coordinator. Although I had been on this journey every step of the way, it wasn't my place to make decisions any longer.

While getting ready to leave for Philadelphia in the middle of the night, I was torn whether to leave my husband alone. He was recovering from a recent bladder cancer surgery and had only been home for a few days. He was too weak to travel. We agreed I should go alone. So, I started out over an hour away from the hospital on a rain slick highway, my heart reaching both forward and back to the men who most needed my care and support.

Hitting the high beams, I hugged the centerline to keep the car from drifting off the road as I traveled in my mind through pictures of decades making this trip with Geoff.

I pictured my infant son safely tucked in his car seat for visits to the hospital three times every week to be poked and prodded by needles and tests. I recalled gazing into the rearview mirror to see the brave toddler playing with action figures. Before I knew it he became the teen-man who courageously faced the monotonous path we traveled so often.

Now, driving alone, I remembered miracles.

The first one that came to mind was on a gray January morning in 1979. I wasn't due to deliver until the following month. That afternoon, I had no symptoms of labor, just a strong sense to get to the hospital right away. Geoff was my ninth pregnancy and the first child for my second husband, Jeff. Because I had a history of miscarriages, I was advised to have an amniocentesis to protect my unborn child. Sadly, no one knew the procedure damaged Geoff's kidneys and that he suffered shock while in the safe place of the womb.

On the day Geoff was to be born, I felt unsettled and dark. I asked my daughter to pray with me. I didn't want my husband to make the long drive in the snow to the hospital if it was a false alarm. But this feeling was deeper than a mother's intuition.

I only know that I felt moved to get to the hospital—then.

Once we arrived, I was rushed from the examining room to the delivery room. The shouts of the doctor chastening the pace of the staff indicated to me there was something very wrong. Dressed in the sterile garb for expectant fathers, Jeff was quickly ushered from the room. Disappointed he would not be able to participate in the birth, he waited anxiously for his first child in the waiting room.

Hours later I woke up on another floor without a swollen body, without a baby. I learned later that my infant had been medivaced to a children's hospital in Philadelphia. The doctor finally came into my room, pulled up a chair close to my bedside, and asked, "How did you know to come to the hospital today, this day, at this time?"

I stared...and stumbled over my words. "I believe the Lord sent me."

The doctor held my hand in hers and said, "I believe He must have."

I was told my baby was only a half hour from being stillborn.

By You I have been sustained from my birth;
You are He who took me from my mother's womb;
My praise is continually of You.
Psalm 71:6

Our baby was in trouble. I was not permitted to leave the hospital for over a week due to hemorrhaging. I wondered if I would ever get to see him. Instead of the joy I anticipated, I remained on the maternity floor among the new moms nursing their babies. I felt a death within my empty insides.

It was challenging for Jeff to balance two hospitals ninety minutes apart and continue to care for our other children at home. Thankfully, my mother and our church family were there to help so he could be with the baby.

At the time, Geoff was the first newborn in the one-hundred-and-four-year history of St Christopher's Hospital for Children to survive dialysis. A form of the procedure had been done unsuccessfully on a small amount of older children. After three months, he was finally able to come home to us. The prognosis was poor. The plan was to wait until he was about four years old before they could explore the possibility of a kidney transplant.

But God works miracles and comes against the words of men. He has a holy flare for the supernatural and extraordinary. I fully believe the unexplained works throughout Geoff's life and before his birth to be actual wonders. Miracles. Medical experts prepared us for certainties that never came to pass. Countless times they told us there was no explanation.

Remembering...

As I continued driving down the dark highway toward the hospital, I was flooded with memories of all the amazing things I had witnessed from this child's birth up until now. I could look back to 1992 when Geoff and I were in our hospital room the night before our surgeries, praying that what was inside of me would allow him to live. It didn't seem like that much time passed before our dear friend, Shirley, knocked at the door to ask if she could do the same thing for him once mine failed in 2002. And then the in-between despair of rejection, waiting lists, and dialysis. Somehow he was able to go on. Because of the power and intervention of an amazing God who never looked away.

Even during this time when he had been living on borrowed time from the last transplanted kidney that was delayed in transport. Only God can make a faulty kidney with limited function preserve a life to catch up to the next miracle.

Gradually his failing body brought us to this day...the long-awaited moment to receive the call that releases the chain of a dialysis chair. And yet, I was fearful this was not what God intended. He had *more and better* waiting.

As the wipers arched across the glass, I prayed, "Lord, if this isn't from You, may it not be." Yet, my peace escaped as I pulled into the parking garage. I knew Jeff must still be lying awake at home, wondering if I arrived safely.

Although I could walk into this hospital blindfolded, I was escorted to where my son was waiting in the pre-surgical unit. Pulling up a chair next to his bedside, it seemed everything was in place except for my assurance. Our understanding was this transplant would be his last, and he was out of options. We were told no one had been transplanted a fourth time in the state of Pennsylvania. So, this final kidney had to be pristine.

I couldn't rid myself of the feeling that this was not the one, not the time...something was wrong.

We prayed together. "Lord, whatever is hidden, please reveal."

Time passed, but stood still. For hours, we gazed at the unopened doors to the operating room where life was waiting on the other side. Finally the transplant surgeon came through the swinging doors. "I'm sorry, we won't be able to go forward with the surgery. For some reason, at the last minute we decided to do a biopsy on this organ. Unfortunately, we found suspicious spongy material." He looked broken as he apologized.

Geoff's glazed eyes watched him exit the room.

I breathed.

We left the hospital distraught and silent. Geoff returned to the dialysis clinic that afternoon while I pulled from the parking garage and headed for home. I asked way too loud in the car, "Father, why have You repeatedly allowed this pain in his life, in our lives?"

My answer came quietly and certain. Nothing had taken me to a more breathtaking elevation in my faith walk than the lengthy journey we had taken together. The little tow-headed boy who had been our joy taught me how to believe in miracles. Yet, I questioned why it had to be in this way.

Times like this brought me to a deep understanding of the story in Genesis 22 when Abraham was called to lay his son on the altar.

Each trip to the hospital has been our journey up Mt. Moriah. Each vigil in the waiting room was my anxious looking among the bushes for the hand of God to provide. I've asked, Will God return my son or take him? Could I continue to love and understand a heavenly Father who allows so much pain?

Like Abraham, I came down from the mountain that day sure of one thing. Through my experiences God had always provided a ram in the thicket and a word of hope. He has shown me His delays are not denials. Sometimes His *no* was simply a loving voice whispering, "Not yet, child. I know better."

Crumbs

We find strength when we understand the goodness of a sovereign God. Otherwise life is totally out of control and we have no hope.

I thank Him for answering my prayer to not allow my son to receive this anticipated kidney because he had the one needed preserved in His storehouse that came later.

Are you waiting for a miracle?

"For nothing is hidden that will not become evident, nor anything secret that will not be known and come to light."
Luke 8:17

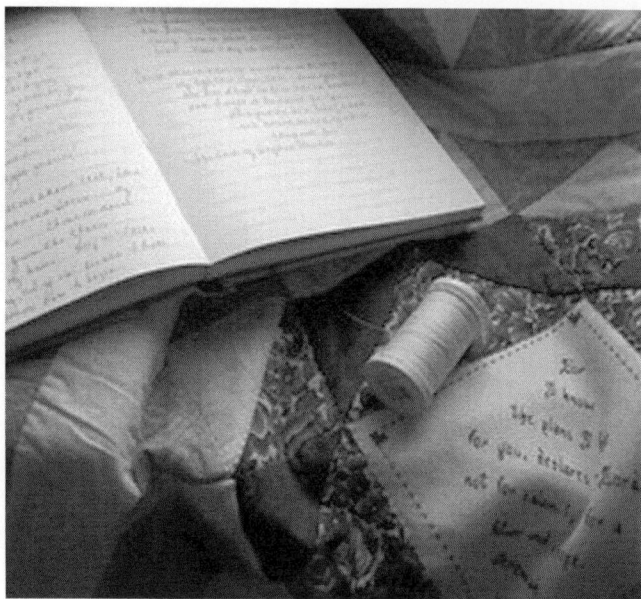

Quilt of Testimony

Promises written in countless journals were stored in a dark drawer as we waited for our son's healing. I wanted to share them with everyone. My daughter and I decided to create a quilt of testimony to tell the story in God's own Word, dated and preserved for a lifetime. The heirloom of grace not only hung in our home, but also displayed in local churches and magazine features.

"This illness is not unto death,
but for the glory of God."
John 11:4 (1979)

And the Child continued to grow and become strong,
increasing in wisdom;
and the grace of God was upon Him.
Luke 2:40 (1979)

By Thee I have been sustained from my birth;
Thou art He who took me from my mother's womb.
Psalm 71:6 (1989)

"Call to Me, and I will answer you,
and I will tell you great and mighty things,
which you do not know."
Jeremiah 33:3 (1992)

"For the vision is yet for the appointed time;
It hastens toward the goal, and it will not fail."
Habakkuk 2:3 (1985-1990)

"Then I will make up to you for the years
that the swarming locust has eaten."
Joel 2:25 (1992)

And the prayer offered in faith will restore
the one who is sick,
and the Lord will raise him up.
James 5:15 (1992)

"For I know the plans that I have for you,"
declares the LORD,
"plans for welfare and not for calamity
to give you a future and a hope."
Jeremiah 29:11 (1992)

"Go your way;
let it be done to you as you have believed."
And the servant was healed that very hour.
Matthew 8:13 (1992)

"And your recovery will speedily spring forth…
The glory of the LORD will be your rear guard.
And you will be like a watered garden,
And like a spring of water whose waters do not fail.
Isaiah 58:8, 11 (1992)

"Come to Me, all who are weary and heavy-laden,
and I will give you rest."
Matthew 11:28 (1992)

The Father of mercies and God of all comfort;
who comforts us in all our affliction
so that we may be able to comfort those
who are in any affliction.
2 Corinthians 1:3–4 (1992)

"By this name, [Jesus],
this man stands before you in good health."
Acts 4:10 (1992)

Now go, write it on a tablet before them
and inscribe it on a scroll, that it may serve
in the time to come as a witness forever.
Isaiah 30:8 (1989)

Crumbs

These precious promises were the Bread of Presence along my path that helped to strengthen me to go on.
I never understood how the God of heaven could speak personally into our lives until I learned to listen during this time.

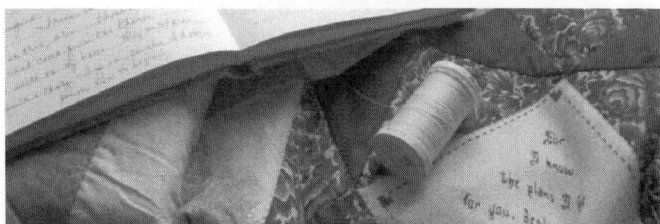

The lost need to be saved,
the saved need to be healed,
and the healed need to be mended.

What do we do when prayer goes unanswered
in the way we expect? In the time we expect?
There is life waiting on the other side of the door
within the healing room, but the door is closed.

Keeper of the Keys

There are times when the long journey doesn't seem to have a destination, simply the same starting place. After a lifetime of illness, I had to face the reality there were no more chances, donors, or hope for my son. It's easy to un-believe while facing impossible situations.

But, I refused. I was still believing and still standing...

From bassinet to multiple hospital bedsides, the constant plea for my son has been, "Please God, one more miracle." Three hundred sixty-five days times thirty-two years equals how many prayers? Yet, I had to believe God was listening and doing what man could not.

I remember the exact stretch of road I was driving on the way home from work when I received a call from the transplant coordinator. "Due to the antibody build up from multiple transplants and years of dialysis, it will be nearly impossible for Geoff to accept another. Less than ten percent living or deceased donors will be compatible at this point."

I was silenced by man's statistics.

All I could hear was the sound of my heart sinking further. Who to believe? The only One I knew I could believe...for wonders.

Meanwhile, I called long-time friend, Sharon, to comfort her after I heard her mother passed away. In spite of her loss, she immediately asked about Geoff. Two years before Sharon offered to donate her kidney for him, but she was quickly denied after the preliminary phone screening. But now, at this urgent time, she wanted to try again to ask if they would reconsider her. Well aware that a donor has to have a compatible blood type and immune system to be considered, we didn't expect the decision to be any different at this time. After testing it was final, Sharon could never be accepted.

However, she was persistent in doing what she could to help Geoff have a full life. She offered to be a part of the newly developed *Paired Exchange* program at the hospital. *Paired Exchange* is an option for recipient and donor pairs who are not blood and tissue compatible. Up until this time, the multi-organ chain was only offered at the distant facility, Johns Hopkins Hospital, that pioneered the process. So, the timing was amazing.

Months of altered schedules and extensive screening didn't get in Sharon's way. Finally, it was determined her kidney would be offered to another in need in order for Geoff to receive from someone who would cross match with him.

But who...and how?

We'll call her Lady Anne, a selfless woman. On one ordinary day while driving to a hair appointment in Philadelphia, she noticed a billboard advertising *The Gift Of Life Center*. After finding the address, she went up to the receptionist and asked if she could speak to someone about saving a life at this special time of the year—Christmas.

When we were told of her generous offer, we were less excited than in the past. The ongoing cycle of hope and despair got in the way of our enthusiasm. We knew this time had to be perfect. *Perfect.* And...would we only get as near as the doorway once again?

Months of testing and anticipation ushered in December. They were compatible! Geoff and his anonymous donor were admitted to two different hospitals. On December 16, 2010, our son was the first in the chain of life at the University of Pennsylvania and one of the first in our state to receive a fourth transplant.

I was silenced by God's supernatural statistics.

A few months later, Sharon and her recipient went to separate regional hospitals to have their procedures. A short time later, donor and recipient families came together at *The Gift of Life* banquet. We finally had the privilege to meet our Good Samaritan donor. No longer anonymous, now announced in newspapers and nightly news stations.

The beauty and blessing of this story isn't simply that someone received life, but that someone sacrificed their comfort and well-being for another. All while a family trusted...in spite of contradicting statistics and evidence.

Lady Anne, by the way, was sixty-five years old at the time. She is responsible for not only saving Geoff's life, but also five others in the multiple chain of life performed in the inner city hospital area. The unending chain continues for more lives to be saved.

Wow—does God's plan trump ours, or what?

We know who holds the keys to the bolted door, finally unlatched by the Keeper of the two appointed keys. Sharon and Anne. One could not open the storehouse of the healing room without the other.

Because His ways...well, are just not our ways...

Do not get discouraged;
it may be the last key in the bunch that opens the door.
Stanisfer

Crumbs

What can I say about this time on my path, except that I was weary with awe. I reread old journals reminding me of God's faithfulness throughout the years, just to hang on...and on.
The stories of healing impossible situations couldn't just be for then, could they? There couldn't be an expiration date on God's power...and there isn't.

What in your life looks impossible?

"I know that You can do everything,
And that no purpose of Yours
can be withheld from You."
Job 42:2 NKJV

The journey is more than a destination,
but without a destination we tend to wander.
Who we are at the end is more important
than who we were at the beginning.

Then and Now

I've shared some of the awe-stops along a journey of messes colliding with miracles. This book has taken longer to write than I thought it would, not because of what is included, but because of what I've chosen to leave out. At times it was harder to write through what has been hard to live through.

But I wanted to know my story. All of it.

Our Father had a biography already written before He placed us in a custom-designed womb for an appointed time here on earth. I believe this. Do you?

Read Psalm 139:16 with me.

Your eyes have seen my unformed substance;
And in Your book were all written
The days that were ordained for me,
When as yet there was not one of them.

No matter your age, you may have noticed that time passes quickly. Sooner than expected, our *then* becomes *now*. So often I've heard, "If I knew then what I know now, life would have been different." True, there are too-many-to-count things I would have done differently, but if I could turn back time, I wouldn't.

Like me, you may think this is definitely not the script you would have written for your life story. Mine would have gone a little like the picket fence version with the perfect husband, perfect kids, peace and plenty, and a dog named Spot.

It didn't happen that way. Not for you, either? Yet, God writes well. When we try and rewrite His story, we get in the way of the main Character.

If only we could edit and delete mistakes and tragedies from the chapters—but then consider the *what if?* I know if I hadn't experienced the then, my now would be very different. I would have passed right by the purpose and lesson stuffed inside of each story and missed the awe and wonder on my path.

I would have missed God.

Quick example. I'm writing this piece during a snowstorm in December while my husband is in the hospital for the fourth time this year. No need to refer to past journals to remember this is the fifth December in a row that he has been admitted for congestive heart failure.

I've learned the hard way that circumstances don't determine our joy, especially during the holiday season. Yet, while shoveling out my car (with arthritic hands!) to get to the hospital, I had to catch myself from falling into the pitiful place of how is my *now* any different than my *then?*

I was weary of the unending cycle. Bone weary.

In the middle of my sorry-this-is-my-story, I received a call from a friend telling me of two deaths within the past three days. One, a young woman my grand-daughter's age, who fought hard against cancer. Suddenly, I was reminded of a saying my husband is quick to quote.

"I cried because I had no shoes until I met a man who had no feet."

One thing that seems to be consistent for every one of us, no matter our path in life—we all have a story to tell about the unique demands placed on us. If we can take inventory of our life, seeing it as *all* good, despite the bitter and the gall, well then, it's a wonderwork of grace in our hearts. It is learning the fine art of sorting treasures from the rubble.

I didn't know my own story until a few years ago when I completed an eye-opening exercise in one of the Beth Moore Bible studies. This wise teacher writes, "God means to be noticed and God means to be remembered."

The process of dividing my life into fifths (from birth to present age) revealed the markers purposely strewn along the God-paved road from my wilderness to promised land. When I prayerfully finished, the scribbles and dots drawn on a line no longer looked like a paper diagram. Instead, it was a masterpiece mural of miracles painted over one big mess.

Suddenly, all the years of journaling my stones of remembrance came to life like a panoramic Polaroid pictorial attached to stories...

Click, a girl swinging high to reach heaven with no one to show her how to get there.

Click, a tattered teen gathering wrong choices along the cracks in the path.

Click, a teen-bride promising forever, too young to promise anything forever.

Click, a young mother listening to her children tell her "Jesus loves you."

Click, after a pat on the soul, believes it.

And that's when God stopped me in my crumb-littered tracks on the same kind of road the apostle Paul was knocked down on and blinded by grace. No longer viewing God as the harsh master staring through the clouds at my every wrong move, I could finally come out from behind the old photos.

There were definitely times while going through the dark, I was tempted to head back for the broad road. When threatening voices whispered despair on every side, the Father taught me how to answer...

I've found someone else. I don't love you anymore.
Some One has found me and will love me forever...

I'm sorry, there's no heartbeat. Your baby has been gone for several weeks.
My miscarried child waits for me in heaven then...

Your child was born with no kidney function. He was a half hour from stillbirth.
Thank You, God, for thirty minutes...

Your son will languish on a waiting list. It's rare to be transplanted four times.
Nothing is impossible with God...

I'm afraid your husband is gone. We'll need to discontinue life support.
We'll wait...

I've lost my job. The medical insurance is too much for the company to cover.
Merry Christmas...

We've lost our home.
The God of heaven will give us success. We will arise and build.

Come quickly, your son has been in a car crash. He's not expected to live.

He will...he will.

I'm afraid he will never walk again.

Yes...he will run.

We're sorry—it's cancer.

Lord, I believe—help my unbelief.

Some stories of brokenness can be told in only a few lines. Any of these crushing events could have prevented me from going on unless I had believed there is a God who can quiet the voice of our circumstances with one holy whisper.

When I first became familiar with the Bible, I found a word just for me, just for you... "I would have despaired unless I had believed that I would see the goodness of the LORD in the land of the living" (Psalm 27:13).

In this Scripture, we're told we can have hope that brings victory, not just in heaven, but here on earth in the land of the living where it's easy to grow faint. Portions of my story remain unanswered, but *I believe I will see* as I have seen, the goodness of the Lord.

Looking back and looking ahead, I ask, What if I never experienced the chaos and grief dressed up in the greatness of a sovereign God? Well then, I could have stayed lost.

How wildly ridiculous, right?

You may feel your story hasn't turned out in the way you would have written and directed, with the cast and crew you would have chosen. But, sweet friend, you can know for sure how it will end.

We have a then, and a now, and a then...just beyond

our last heartbeat is eternity. That's where our Savior has pointed all along the way, waiting for us to catch up to follow Him.

My prayer is that you recognize the crumbs scattered on your personal journey have been placed on purpose to lead you to the safe destination of Jesus.

*At the end of life, our well-written stories
will lay before the Father's feet.
May He look to the right where His Son sits,
and whisper, "She believed."*

and after...

In the beginning of the journey, would I have gone willingly if the Lord said, "Come and go to these hard places with Me"? I doubt it. But I'm glad the answer became yes, if it means being with Him forever. And it does.

I would feel like I left you in the middle of the road if I didn't ask you to join me. When we're not sure where we're going, nothing feels more comforting than to find someone who is familiar with the road that leads home. If you don't know how to begin your journey, or get off the one you've been on, I've found the way... His name is Jesus.

Many times I've been questioned about my relationship with the Lord, by those who believe, and those who don't. They want to know what drew me, kept me, and caused me to continue to believe. I'd love to communicate something grand, but I only know to say, *I listened hard, and I believed what I heard.*

The Word of God.

If you're not sure of your relationship with Jesus, I encourage you to look for Him in the Bible, seek out a local church that preaches the true gospel, and find someone who will disciple you well.

For all have sinned and fall short of the glory of God.
Romans 3:23

You can receive Jesus into your life...right now. You only need to realize you are a sinner who needs to be rescued.

Many of us don't like the word *sinner* and feel no need to be rescued. We feel we can do it on our own.

If we could, we would.

The Bible teaches if we confess with our mouth that Jesus is Lord, trust and believe He is the Son of God who came to earth to die for our sins, then we have an eternal home with Him in heaven.

"For God so loved the world,
that He gave His only begotten Son,
that whoever believes in Him shall not perish,
but have eternal life.
John 3:16

May this day be the day you surrender your life to the One who can change it. It doesn't mean tomorrow will be without problems and pressures, but it does mean life is changed in spite of what is happening.

I hope that sharing my stories has inspired you to see Jesus on every page of your own story.

Follow the crumbs, and I believe that we'll meet someday,

Verna

*A journal is the archived landscape of your life
drawn with words. Writing down the journey
uncovers the beauty that we often overlook.*

Journaling the Journey

There is no sweeter time than the still of the morning when I meet with the Father. It's quiet. Not a sound but the purr of my cat nestling tight to my side in the overstuffed prayer-chair. Life is good, having a little daybreak therapy as I pray with my pen.

But then...

The day gets in the way and my journal is nothing more than random jots scribbled on a tattered scrap to be transcribed at a later time into my book of remembrance.

King David and I have spent many quiet dawns and silent nights in the book of Psalms. *A man after God's own heart* records an honest account of failed flesh and flaws for all to read. The ancient journal penned from a sheep pasture to a palatial palace reveals his helplessness and praise. Mine does, too.

Recording my spiritual journey is one experience that has changed my life. I have baskets of journals filled with manna-crumbs that I've gathered to remind me that God has been there the whole time.

I encourage you to begin a devotional journal and see beautiful changes in your relationship with Jesus.

You might say, "I don't know where to begin. I don't have the time. I don't know how to write, and I don't have anything to say."

Or you might ask, why journal?

A benefit of journaling is how it strengthens our faith and helps us discover more than ourselves. God tells us in His Word to remember. Memories fade, so the best way to remember what He has done is to *write His answers* down.

What about the things that get in the way?

I don't know where to begin. Begin with the first step. Get alone with your Bible, pen, and a blank book where God's voice can fill in the white space.

I don't have time. Start out small. Spend the first few moments in prayer. If you need a formula to order your steps, take ten minutes to read, ten minutes to write, and ten minutes to pray. As one day turns into a week, into a month, it will soon become a holy habit and you'll no longer look at the time.

I don't know how to write. Certainly, you do. Skip the grammar and punctuation and simply free-write. You're not writing to impress anyone. It's between you and your pen.

I don't have anything to say. Just write your heart and expect the Lord to visit your sacred place. You may find it helpful to use the questions at the end of each story to begin your journey.

And if you care to go deeper, you can ask yourself:

What do I believe about my situation?
What do I believe about God?
What does God say I can believe?

Before long, you'll have a journal that is a treasured keepsake.

Now it's your turn to write your story.

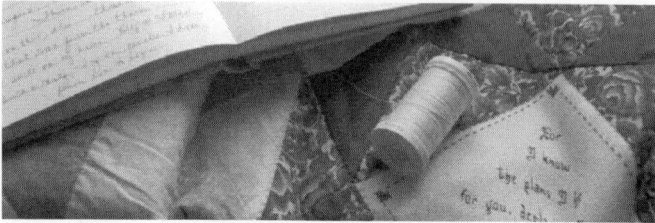

*It is in being real by telling our story
that others can look inside their own story.*

Acknowledgements

It took a long time to finally come to the place where I could write my stories down for others to read. The words were kept safe in my journals. It only became possible when God provided those who stood close by, advised, motivated, and loved me through it.

And each one, I acknowledge gratefully:

• My husband, Jeff. You patiently and tirelessly lived out much of the story alongside me. You were the one holding my bag of rocks so I could take one more step. And then, just as patiently and tirelessly re-lived the stories while proofreading every one. I so appreciate you!

• My children. Thank you for allowing me to share your part of my story so others could have hope. I am forever grateful to my first born(s) Sherise and Tom, who brought me to the Lord, and to my last born(s) Shane and Geoff, for keeping me there. A special thanks to you, dear daughter, for helping me find the hidden crumbs.

• My grandchildren, Japheth, Rachel, Joah, Taleh, Brianna, Avery...for simply living and giving me hope.

• My editor, encourager, mentor, dear friend, and publisher, Marlene Bagnull. You taught me how to "write His answer" through years of excellent writers conferences. I can't find words to express my deep-heart gratitude for taking me under your experienced, generous, and patient wing. The Lord was extravagant when He gave you the gift of encouragement.

• My more-than-a-critique-group. Your tough love and skill pulled out the deep and the dark. I am especially grateful to Lori Hynson and Carolyn Ruch, my "therapists." The two of you will go down in my history. The Lord knit us together through our stories, for such a time as this.

• My more-than-a-friend, Sue Landis. You are not only my life coach, but the birth coach who helped in this laborious process from conception to delivery. You were the best accountability partner! If not for you, I would have come down from the mountain with blank pages.

• My more-than-a-friend, Karen Kutzner. You are the articulate one who makes sense of my random language. How many titles did we come up with? No matter how long I tarried, you never gave up on me. I love you for believing in me.

• My more-than-a-friend, Glenda Mills. You have been my strong encourager, not only while writing the stories, but while living many of them out. I would have called it a day if you had not prayed me through another twenty-four hours.

• My forever-friend, Rose Sweeney. Thank you, child-hood friend, who knows me from the inside-out and loves me anyway. You could write my story without me.

• My Precept sisters. Together, we kneel, laugh, cry, fast, feast, and study God's Word every Thursday morning. Thank you for being the precious crumbs on my path for over twenty-five years. Greek for gratitude; eucharisteo #2169

• My sheltering friends at Immanuel Leidy's Church. You, dear family, are the prayer warriors who have stood by me in battle. You are in-between the lines of many of my stories.

• Everlasting gratitude to our old Bible study gang. Thank each one of you for writing deep stories into our hearts. Shirley and Sharon, I am forever grateful for your amazing sacrificial gift to my son.

• A special thank you to Jo Lauter and Marlene Bagnull for cover design, and, Verity, my "cover girl." And a special thank you to my critique-pal, Christy Distler, for the excellent proofreading.

• Eddie Jones. You helped me turn one story into ten with one simple formula. You told me I could write when I had a cast on my hand—and a cast on my pen. Thank you!

• And not last, but forever, my parents who loved me well.

• *Mostly...I gratefully acknowledge, my Jesus. If I could lay one manuscript before Your holy feet, it would be the one You wrote for me.*

You make known to me the path of life;
you will fill me with joy
in your presence.

Psalm 16:11

May our paths cross someday, kind friend.
I hope you will visit my website
where I share, one story at a time,
the crumbs along my path
that are leading me closer to Jesus.

vernabowman.com

I am available to speak
at your women's ministry event.

Please contact me at
gvbowman@comcast.net
215-237-1370

We were so blessed to have you.
The retreat evaluations were awesome!
You touched so many hearts. You're an inspiration!

Marlene Mayle, Ministry Leader
First Baptist Church
Grafton, West Virginia
March 2014

Made in the USA
San Bernardino, CA
25 April 2014